SOCIALIST WELFARE IN A MARKET ECONOMY

Socialist Welfare in a Market Economy

Social security reforms in Guangzhou, China

NELSON CHOW
University of Hong Kong

YEUBIN XU
China Civil Affairs Cadres Training Institute

Routledge
Taylor & Francis Group
LONDON AND NEW YORK

First published 2001 by Ashgate Publishing

Reissued 2018 by Routledge
2 Park Square, Milton Park, Abingdon, Oxon OX14 4RN
711 Third Avenue, New York, NY 10017, USA

Routledge is an imprint of the Taylor & Francis Group, an informa business

A Library of Congress record exists under LC control number: 2001086235

ISBN 13: 978-1-138-71698-8 (hbk)
ISBN 13: 978-1-315-19676-3 (ebk)

Contents

List of Tables

Foreword

China decided to adopt an open-door policy in 1978 and since then its economy has been making remarkable progress. Studies and, hence, books and articles on the successful story of economic development in China are not difficult to come by as there are certainly lessons that other developing countries would like to learn. While these books and articles have not totally ignored the impacts of the economic reforms on the livelihood of the Chinese people, attention was mainly given to the improvements in living standard.

The achievements that China has made in uplifting the living standard of her people should no doubt be applauded. They are even more remarkable when one considers the fact that economic reforms have only started for just over twenty years, and during this period, the extent of poverty has drastically been reduced. What is intriguing is that China, as a socialist country, has achieved all these by first welcoming foreign investments and later by openly adopting a market economy. No wonder queries have been raised, by critics both outside and inside, about whether China has forsaken its socialist ideology or not? The answer given by the Chinese leaders is that as long as the reforms bring in progress, China is on the right way to develop its own form of socialism.

In order to justify that China remains socialist, the Chinese leaders have been conscious to maintain the dominant role of the state-owned enterprises. The state-owned enterprises are important because, as a socialist country, the Chinese government can never let go of the control of the means of production. It also cannot let down the employees of the state-owned enterprises who, for a long time since the founding of the Republic, have depended on the country for their support and protection. Hence, when the Chinese government announced its intention to turn the state-owned enterprises into modern ones, the decision was as shocking as that for adopting a market economy. Employees of the state-owned enterprises, who still constitute the majority of the urban labour force, understood that their 'iron rice bowl' and the protection that they used to enjoy, would soon be cracked, if not broken into pieces.

This book examines the reforms that China has carried out in its state-owned enterprises and the associated labour and welfare systems. It is the product of a study that the authors have carried out, in the latter part of the 1990s, on social welfare development in Guangzhou, the most populous city in southern China. There is no intention to map out here every detail of the changes that state-owned enterprises in Guangzhou have undergone, as well as that in their social security provisions. The focus is on how these enterprises have responded to the call to make them competitive in the market and, at the same time, honour their promises to provide for the welfare of their employees.

Even with this limited objective, we have found the study not an easy one. There are several limitations that we have to accept. First, we tried to understand what has happened at the central level as well as what has actually been implemented in Guangzhou, since it is still imperative for local governments in China to adhere to what has been decided centrally. While central directives are readily available, as they can easily be found in announcements and decisions of the State Council and concerned government departments, information on their application at the municipal level is often missing. We have to construct the picture from the various channels that we are able to get hold of. Though we are certain that our findings on the Guangzhou situation, presented in Part Three, should be very close to what has actually happened, there are bound to be gaps that we are unable to close.

Second, as we have mentioned several times in the book, Guangzhou is in fact not representative of other cities in China. We have taken Guangzhou as our case to study because we have the full co-operation of the Guangzhou Academy of Social Sciences and we have benefited a lot from our discussions with their researchers. Notwithstanding the fact that the Guangzhou experience is a non-typical one, we understand that what happened in Guangzhou often became an example for other cities in China to follow. In this way, the study of social security reforms in Guangzhou is a worthwhile attempt.

Third, though we have tried to link up, as far as possible, the reform of state-owned enterprises with that of their social security obligations, the two are not necessarily interrelated with one another. We have to accept that reforms in each area would have their own justifications and it is not easy to say which comes first and has a higher priority.

This book is divided into four parts and twelve chapters. Part One examines in detail the changes that have taken place in the state-owned enterprises, particularly the labour and wage system, since economic reforms started in 1978. Part Two focuses the discussions on two of the most important social security obligations of the state-owned enterprises, namely old-age pensions and unemployment benefits. Part Three takes Guangzhou as an example and examines the relationship between the reforms of the state-owned enterprises and the changes in their social security provisions. The final part is a brief discussion of the observations that have arisen from our study.

Ever since the beginning of the economic reforms in China, and hence the reforms of the state-owned enterprises, there is always the question whether or not China can maintain its socialist welfare system. There is certainly no ready answer, but we hope that this book can contribute to a better understanding of this seemingly didactic question.

Acknowledgements

This book comes out of a study on social welfare in Guangzhou, the most populous city in southern China and one of the first cities in China to go into market economy. We would like to acknowledge the assistance of the Guangzhou Academy of Social Sciences, our collaborator in the study. The study has been made possible with a sumptuous grant from the Research Grants Council of the Government of the Hong Kong Special Administrative Region of the People's Republic of China. Finally we would like to thank the people, whose names are too numerous to mention here, who have assisted us in the course of conducting this study and given us valuable advice.

PART ONE

ECONOMIC AND LABOUR REFORMS IN CHINA

1 Economic Growth and the Diminishing Role of State-owned Enterprises

Diversification of the Economy

China has impressed the world for its continued high growth rates since economic reforms started in 1978. Over the past two decades, gross domestic product (GDP) in China grew from 362.41 billion yuan in 1978 to 7,939.57 billion yuan in 1998, with annual growth rate averaging around 10 per cent (*China Statistical Yearbook 1999*, p. 57). Per capita GDP also increased from 379 yuan in 1978 to 6,392 yuan in 1998. Although the growth rate began to slow down since the early 1990s, decreasing from 14.2 per cent in 1992 to 7.8 per cent in 1998, China has continued to register an annual growth rate higher than most developing countries.

Rapid economic growth is also reflected in the gross industrial output value (GIOV). The GIOV increased from 515.4 billion yuan in 1980 to 11,904.8 billion yuan in 1998, with an average annual growth rate at 13.2 per cent between 1986 and 1990, 22.2 per cent between 1991 and 1995, and 18.8 per cent between 1991 and 1998 (*China Statistical Yearbook 1999*, pp. 22-23). What is even more significant is the improvement in the living standard of the people, represented by the increase in the per capita annual disposable income of urban households, which rose from 343.4 yuan in 1978 to 5,425.1 yuan in 1998. Table 1.1 gives the situation of GDP, per capita GDP, GIOV and per capita disposable income of urban households in China between 1978 and 1998.

Throughout the reform period starting from 1978, diversification has no doubt been the most distinguishing feature of social and economic planning in China. One can even say that the process of economic reforms in China has been one of economic and labour force diversification. In making the transition from a centrally planned economy to a socialist market economy, reforms have turned the traditionally single public-ownership economy, which consisted almost exclusively of stated-owned enterprises and collectively owned enterprises, into a mixture of miscellaneous systems with various types of ownership and managerial forms. At present, the current urban economic system in China can be divided into four different sub-systems, according to the nature of ownership: (1) state-owned enterprises (SOEs), including enterprises with the state holding the controlling share; (2) collectively owned enterprises; (3) individually owned enterprises; and (4) enterprises with other types of ownership, including joint ventures, shareholding corporations, foreign-funded enterprises, and enterprises funded by residents from Hong Kong, Macao and Taiwan.

Table 1.1: GDP, per capita GDP, GIOV and per capita disposable income of urban residents in China, 1978-98

Year	GDP (billion yuan)	Per capita GDP (yuan)	GIOV (billion yuan)	Per capita disposable income of urban households (yuan)
1978	362.41	379	423.7	343.4
1979	403.82	417	–	–
1980	451.78	460	515.4	477.6
1981	486.24	489	–	–
1982	529.47	525	–	–
1983	593.45	580	–	–
1984	717.10	692	–	–
1985	896.44	853	971.6	739.1
1986	1,020.22	956	–	899.6
1987	1,196.25	1,104	–	1,002.2
1988	1,492.83	1,355	–	1,181.4
1989	1,690.92	1,512	–	1,375.7
1990	1,854.79	1,634	2,392.4	1,510.2
1991	2,161.78	1,879	2,662.5	1,700.6
1992	2,663.81	2,287	3,459.9	2,026.6
1993	3,463.44	2,939	4,840.2	2,577.4
1994	4,675.94	3,923	7,017.6	3,496.2
1995	5,847.81	4,854	9,189.4	4,283.0
1996	6,788.46	5,576	9,959.5	4,838.9
1997	7,446.26	6,053	11,373.3	5,160.3
1998	7,939.57	6,392	11,904.8	5,425.1

Sources: 'China Statistical Yearbook 1999', p. 55, for GDP and per capita GDP; p. 423, for GIOV; and p. 318, for per capita disposable income of urban residents.

–: Information not available.

Growth of the Non-state Sector

Since reforms started in 1978, economic development in China has been one of the re-emergence and rapid growth of the non-state sector, particularly individually owned enterprises and enterprises with other types of ownership. For instance, GIOV for individually owned enterprises increased, between 1980 and 1998, from 100 million yuan to 2,037.2 billion yuan. GIOV also increased, during the same period, from 2.4 billion yuan to 2,727 billion yuan for enterprises with other types of ownership, and from 121.3 billion yuan to 4,573 billion yuan for collectively owned enterprises (*China Statistical Yearbook 1999*, p. 423). However, GIOV of SOEs increased only from 391.6 billion yuan in 1980 to 3,617.3 billion yuan in 1996, and since then declined steadily to 3,362.1 billion yuan in 1998. It should be pointed out that many of the collectively owned enterprises were in fact operated with private investment and ownership, and they were registered as collectively owned enterprises because in the early days of economic reforms, private ownership was still politically unacceptable.

To put it another way, of the 515.4 billion yuan of GIOV in 1980, SOEs made up 75.98 per cent, collectively owned enterprises 23.54 per cent, and the non-public sector (including individually owned enterprises and enterprises with other types of ownership) accounted for only 0.49 per cent. After nearly two decades of economic reforms, of the 11,904.8 billion yuan of GIOV in 1998, SOEs produced 28.24 per cent, 38.41 per cent by collectively owned enterprises, and over 40 per cent by the non-public sector. Table 1.2 presents the situation of GIOV in China between 1978 and 1998 by types of ownership.

Table 1.2: GIOV in China by types of ownership, 1978-98 (billion yuan)

Year	Total GIOV	By SOEs	By collectively owned enterprises	By individually owned enterprises	By enterprises with other types of ownership
1978	423.7	328.9	94.8	–	–
1979	–	–	–	–	–
1980	515.4	391.6	121.3	0.1	2.4
1981	–	–	–	–	–
1982	–	–	–	–	–
1983	–	–	–	–	–
1984	–	–	–	–	–
1985	971.6	630.2	311.7	18.0	11.7
1986	–	–	–	–	–
1987	–	–	–	–	–
1988	–	–	–	–	–
1989	–	–	–	–	–
1990	2,392.4	1,306.4	852.3	129.0	104.7
1991	2,662.5	1,495.5	878.3	128.7	160.0
1992	3,459.9	1,782.4	1,213.5	200.6	263.4
1993	4,840.2	2,272.5	1,646.4	386.1	535.2
1994	7,017.6	2,620.1	2,647.2	708.2	1,042.1
1995	9,189.4	3,122.0	3,362.3	1,182.1	1,523.1
1996	9,959.5	3,617.3	3,923.2	1,542.0	1,658.2
1997	11,373.3	3,596.8	4,334.7	2,037.6	2,098.2
1998	11,904.8	3,362.1	4,573.0	2,037.2	2,727.0

Sources: 'China Statistical Yearbook 1999', p. 55 for GDP and per capita GDP; p. 423 for GIOV; and p. 318 for per capita disposable income of urban residents.

–: Information not available.

With the diversification of the economy, the traditional permanent worker system has gradually disappeared. Within the urban labour force, those who work in state-owned and collectively owned economic units, as well as other types of ownership, are usually referred to as formal employees. In other words, formal employees would not include re-employed retirees, private entrepreneurs, workers in private enterprises, the self-employed, workers in village and township enterprises, agricultural labourers, foreign workers, and workers from Hong Kong, Macao, and Taiwan, all of whom are often simply classified as employees. In the past two decades, particularly since the mid-1990s, increases in the number of employees in the cities have mainly been a phenomenon of the non-state sector.

From 1978 to 1998, the number of urban employees rose steadily from 95.14 million to 206.78 million. In terms of the ownership of the enterprises, the number of urban employees in SOEs increased from 74.51 million in 1978 to 112.61 million in 1995, and then declined steadily to 90.58 million in 1998. Those in collectively owned enterprises increased from 20.48 million in 1978 to 36.28 million in 1991, and then decreased consistently to 19.63 million in 1998 (*China Statistical Yearbook 1999*, p. 136). In contrast, between 1985 and 1998, the number of urban employees in enterprises with non-state ownership rose steadily from 0.38 million to 48.97 million.

It should further be noted that while the number of formal employees grew from 94.99 million in 1978 to 149.08 million in 1995, it then decreased to 123.37 million in 1998 (*China Statistical Yearbook 1999*, p. 140). Out of the 123.37 million formal employees by the end of 1998, in terms of the types of ownership, 88.09 million worked in state-owned economic units, 19 million in collectively owned economic units and 16.28 million in economic units with other types of ownership. In terms of the types of organization, 86.12 million worked in enterprises, 26.76 million in public institutions and 10.48 million as government workers (*China Statistical Yearbook 1999*, p. 142).

The change in the employment pattern of urban employees clearly indicates that the impact of the economic reforms is most deeply felt among workers working in SOEs. And one should remember that in urban China, the kind of enterprise where one works determines to a large extent the wage and benefits he or she receives. As economic reforms are gradually taking away the traditional employment security and privileges of the employees in the SOEs, the road of economic reforms becomes to them also one to insecurity.

2 Reform of State-owned Enterprises: A Historical Overview

The Three Stages of Economic Reform

Between the founding of the People's Republic of China (PRC) in 1949 and up to 1978, China had adopted a centrally planned economy for most of the time. During this period, public ownership was the only type of ownership in the cities. The government decided over what and how to be produced by SOEs through centrally decided plans, with profits handed over to and losses covered by the state. Under the central planning mechanism, enterprises had little autonomy over their economic activities. Their primary concern was to fulfill the production quotas set by higher authorities and they were neither concerned with nor in a position to seek profit. In a word, SOEs in the planned economy era were not profit-seeking economic entities; they were merely workshops to implement centrally set policies.

To invigorate SOEs, China started to reform its economic system as early as 1978. Reform policies have been carried out with great caution and incrementally, characterized by experimentation in design and gradualism in implementation (World Bank, 1997). While rural economic reforms in China were initiated from the bottom, SOEs reforms have been taking a top-down approach. As such, SOEs reforms in the past two decades in China have undergone three very distinct stages. In the first stage, which spanned approximately between 1978 and 1984, the efforts of the government were to transform the status of SOEs from workshops of the government into independent economic entities. In this period, SOEs were given increasing autonomy over production and management, and were made responsible for profits and losses.

The second stage spanned between 1985 and 1992. The focus of SOEs reforms during this period was to explore ways of 'separating government from enterprises'. In practice, it took the form of 'separating ownership from management'. From 1993 onwards, SOEs reforms moved to its third stage. The dominant theme in this stage has been to build modern enterprises in China. However, as a result of the economic drawbacks since the end of 1997, SOEs reforms have somewhat slackened, with the efforts of the government concentrating on relieving SOEs of economic difficulties.

1979-84: Decentralization of Authority and Returning Profits to Enterprises

Following the Third Plenary Session of the Eleventh Central Committee Meeting of the Chinese Communist Party (CCP) in 1978, nation-wide SOEs reforms in China started on a trial-before-promotion basis, with 'decentralization of authority and returning profits to enterprises' and 'taxation replacing profits' as slogans. In July 1979, the State Council issued five documents to reform state-owned industrial enterprises, requiring local governments to select SOEs for experiments on expanding the autonomy of the enterprises.

As the focus of the reform was to readjust the relationship between the state and SOEs over the distribution of profits, SOEs were thus given greater autonomy in production, distribution, and management. To be specific, SOEs were allowed to retain a certain percentage of profits and use them as funds for development, welfare and bonuses. They were also given the authority over the use of the retained funds, after fulfilling the quotas set by the state, to make supplementary production plans according to individual situations, to develop new products, handle exports, manage their own labour force, and design new administrative structures.

By the end of 1980, the number of SOEs selected for experiment amounted to 6,000, representing about 16 per cent of the state-owned industrial enterprises. In 1981, the economic responsibility system was introduced, and was later widely adopted in all state-owned industrial enterprises throughout the country. By the end of 1981, over 42,000 state-owned industrial enterprises adopted various forms of economic responsibility system.

'Taxation replacing profits' was another important measure in reforming SOEs. In April 1983, the State Council approved 'An Announcement on Trial Methods for Taxation Replacing Profits in SOEs' prepared by the Ministry of Finance, and commonly known as the first step of 'taxation replacing profits'. According to the document, the former practice of SOEs handing over profits to the state was replaced by the state imposing taxes on SOEs. However, the practice of requiring profitable enterprises to hand over a portion of their profits to the state had not immediately stopped, resulting in some SOEs paying both taxes and profits to the state. In September 1984, the State Council approved 'An Announcement on Carrying out the Second Step of Taxation Replacing

Profits in SOEs' prepared by the Ministry of Finance, by which SOEs handing over both profits and taxes to the state was thoroughly replaced by taxation alone.

In May 1984, the State Council issued 'Regulations on Further Expanding the Autonomy of Enterprises'. The document gave SOEs autonomy in ten areas such as making production plans, sales, pricing, purchasing, using funds, arranging for production, designing administrative structure, personnel and labour management, designing the remunerative system, and engaging in joint ventures. Following the Third Plenary Session of the Twelfth Central Committee Meeting of the CCP in October 1984, which stipulated that the focus of economic reforms in the cities was to invigorate enterprises, the autonomy of SOEs continued to be expanded.

Alongside with the experiment on expanding the autonomy of the SOEs, reforms were simultaneously made in the macro-economic environment. Top-down state plan directives were gradually replaced by economic regulations, emphasizing the use of prices and markets. Other characteristics of the socialist economy, such as price-fixing and state planning in production, allocation of production means, procurement and investment, were no more stressed. Through these reform measures, SOEs obtained different degrees of autonomy in production and management. To a large extent, the former tight control of the government over SOEs was relaxed, and SOEs began to move in the direction of becoming relatively independent economic entities.

However, the principle that 'the planned economy is the principal form and that market adjustment is only supplementary' was still adhered to and reform measures could at best be regarded as attempts to tinker with the economic system. Furthermore, owing to the fact that the management and ownership of SOEs had not effectively been separated during this period, the operation of the SOEs continued to rely heavily on the government, and their autonomy was often limited to the distribution process. As a result, economic behaviours of the SOEs were often characterized by short-term objectives, such as increasing wages for employees and offering them bonuses in abusive ways.

1985-92: Separating Government from Enterprises

In 1984, the Third Plenary Session of the Twelfth Central Committee Meeting of the CCP passed 'Decisions of the Party Central Committee on Implementing Reform Policies in the Economic System'. The central government decided to turn SOEs into truly independent production and management entities, and stipulated that enterprises must be responsible for their own profits and losses. To accomplish this goal, the central government called for local governments to explore and experiment on ways of 'separating government from enterprises' or 'separating ownership from management'.

The autonomy of SOEs was further affirmed and expanded following the Third Plenary Session of the Twelfth Central Committee Meeting of the CCP, which recognized that effective separation of ownership from management heavily depended on the extent to which enterprises could be given autonomy in production and management. Since 1984, SOEs reforms in China moved on to the experiment of various forms of management responsibility systems, of which contracts and leasing became two of the major methods to accomplish the goal. The common practice was that large and medium-size SOEs would adopt the contracts system while small ones would be leased out. Enterprises operated under the contracts system were allowed to retain the surplus profits after they had fulfilled the contracted quotas, but they had also to cover any losses by themselves. By the end of 1987, about 80 per cent of state-owned industrial enterprises adopted the contracts system. In 1991, over 90 per cent of the previously contracted enterprises signed the second round of contracts. In the following years, the government made further efforts to improve and perfect the contracts system.

In 1988, the National People's Congress passed 'Law of State-owned Industrial Enterprises of the PRC', which is commonly referred to as the Enterprise Law. Enterprises were defined in the Enterprise Law as 'socialist commodities producing and managing units' which operate with autonomy in management, are responsible for profits and losses, and maintain independent accounting procedures. To facilitate the separation of ownership from management, the Enterprise Law legalized and extended the autonomy of enterprises to virtually all aspects of their operation. Enterprises were allowed to adopt responsibility systems in such areas as contracting and leasing, production, distribution, personnel management, design of administrative and management structures, purchasing materials, selling of products under the guidelines of the state plan, and recruiting and dismissing of employees according to relevant regulations. The Enterprise Law also stipulated that managers must assume full responsibilities for the operation of their enterprises.

In 1992, the State Council issued 'Regulations on the Transformation of Managerial Mechanism in State-owned Industrial Enterprises'. The regulations reaffirmed and extended the rights of enterprises as independent economic entities as were stipulated in the Enterprise Law, re-emphasized that enterprises must be responsible for losses due to poor performance, re-defined the owner-trustee relationship between the government and enterprises, and finally outlined the legal responsibilities that government and enterprises each would have to bear if they failed to perform adequately. While the regulations continued to be focused on defining the relationship between the government and enterprises, subsequent SOEs reforms began to give more attention to reforming the operational mechanism of the enterprises.

1993- : The Establishment of Modern Enterprises

With the removal of ideological barriers following the speech made by Deng Xiao-ping in 1992, economic reforms in China took on new momentum. In 1992, the Second Plenary Session of the Fourteenth Central Committee Meeting of the CCP defined, for the first time, that the goal of economic reforms in China was the establishment of a socialist market economy. In 1993, the Third Plenary Session of the Fourteenth Central Committee Meeting of the CCP passed 'Decisions on the Establishment of a Socialist Market Economy', in which the goal of SOEs reforms was broadly defined as the establishment of a modern enterprise system. The decisions defined the modern enterprise system as having four characteristics: (1) non-ambiguity in asset ownership; (2) clearly defined rights and responsibilities; (3) government separating from enterprises; and (4) the employment of scientific management. Since 1993, SOEs reforms in China have been emphasizing the reform of the government-enterprise relationship and the restructuring of the internal managerial mechanism as two of the important elements in the establishment of modern enterprises.

In practice, the task of establishing modern enterprises has been to turn enterprises into shareholding companies or corporations with board of directors representing investors and managers managing the businesses. Major methods employed would include: (1) transformation of SOEs into share-holding or limited-liability companies with multiple shareholders or investors; (2) transformation of administrative agencies or bureaus into shareholding companies with the state holding the controlling share; and (3) restructuring SOEs through close-downs, mergers, change of the production line, or declaring bankruptcy. In 1995, the State Council selected 100 SOEs, with local governments selecting 2,343 ones, for experiments on establishing modern enterprises. By the end of 1996, 98 of the 100 national experiment spots, and over 85 per cent of the local ones, went through transformation or restructuring (Zhou, 1998). In the following years, while the government has been making continued efforts to improve the experiment spots, SOEs reforms have been expanded nation-wide with the slogan of 'focusing attention on large SOEs and invigorating small ones'. In actual terms, the State Council selected 580 national key SOEs, and made extensive efforts to insure that they would perform well or protect them from going into bankruptcy, while small SOEs would be allowed to be sold, merged or privatized.

In summary, coming to the end of the twentieth century, and after the three phases of economic reforms, SOEs in China have largely been turned into modern enterprises, with the primary purpose of pursuing profits. There is no doubt that the state still holds tight control over the SOEs and there is also not a lack of state plans or directives for SOEs to follow, but SOEs, on the other hand, have gradually become independent economic entities. Furthermore, together with the transformation of the SOEs from merely economic tools in the hands of the state to modern enterprises with their own production and marketing strategies, the relationship between the enterprises and their employees has also changed, which will be topics of discussion in later chapters.

3 Reform of the Labour and Wage System

Permanent to Contractual Employment

An important component of SOEs reforms in China is the reform of the labour system. During the planned economy era, China adopted a permanent labour system in the state sector for most of the time. Under this system, workers were assigned to enterprises by the state according to state plans, and their employment was usually on a permanent basis. Employees and employers could not select each other. They were put together through unified arrangements by the state and labour mobility was extremely limited. Enterprises could not refuse to accept workers they did not need, nor could they dismiss those whom they found unsatisfactory. By the same token, workers who had been assigned to a work unit would often remain in the same unit until they retired, and they did not have the freedom of changing their employers. Under this system, both the morale of employees and the efficiency of enterprises were negatively affected.

After the inception of the economic reforms, the system of permanent labour became a conspicuous problem. With the purpose of creating a labour system under which both enterprises and employees could make mutual selections, the government began to reform the labour system in various localities of China in 1978. Reforms began with the expansion of the employment channels.

Unlike the previous practice that the labour department was the only channel through which employment could be arranged, local governments were encouraged to provide jobs for the unemployed, who were then called ‘people waiting for employment’, either through local labour departments or by people running private businesses. Furthermore, in order to create employment opportunities for an influx of young people returning to the cities, the government actively promoted the development of collectively owned enterprises, such as labour service companies and other types of economic activities with private owners responsible for their profits and losses.

Meanwhile, contractual employment was applied to newly recruited employees in state and collectively owned enterprises on an experimental basis. In 1986, the State Council issued a document, formally establishing the system of contract labour. The document stipulated that new employees have to be employed on a contractual basis with clearly defined rights and obligations between employers and employees, and thus put a stop to the previously centrally planned labour system. After that, government ceased to assign employment quotas to enterprises, allowing the latter to recruit employees on contractual, temporary or seasonal bases according to individual needs. Following the establishment of the contractual labour system, permanent employees were also gradually brought under the same contractual basis in order to invigorate the enterprises. In 1994, the National People's Congress passed the Labour Law, in which the contractual labour system was legalized, and has since been applied to all types of employees and enterprises.

The implementation of the contractual labour system had, in the early years of implementation, made little impact upon the status of permanent employees because the new system applied only to newly recruited workers. Permanent workers continued to enjoy what was called the 'iron rice bowls', meaning a secure job. It was in the mid-1990s, with the ongoing of SOEs reforms, that fundamental changes were brought to the permanent labour system. As SOEs becoming more independent, enterprises were encouraged to introduce internal reforms by adopting such measures as 'contractual administration', 'optimizing regrouping' and 'merit employment' to rectify the drawbacks of the permanent labour system and to shed off surplus employees.

Under the 'contractual administration' arrangement, permanent workers would be required to sign contracts with their enterprises, specifying the right and responsibilities of each. The 'optimizing regrouping' arrangement would require permanent workers to resign first and then re-employed in order to improve efficiency. The 'merit employment' arrangement would award re-employed permanent workers based on their performance. In short, the employment of these methods was to allow enterprises to restructure their labour force to increase efficiency. As under-employment was a conspicuous phenomenon for most SOEs, regrouping of labour in this way led to many permanent employees losing their jobs. Surplus labour began to emerge in China and the 'iron rice bowl' was no longer unbreakable.

Growth of Employment in the Non-state Sector

Another consequence of the economic reforms was that employment became increasingly diversified and complex. Thus, at the end of 1997, of the 202.07 million urban employees, 146.68 million worked in state-owned and collectively owned enterprises, 1.33 million as employees in private enterprises, 10.24 million as self-employed industrial and commercial households, 26.69 million in private enterprises and self-employed households, and 17.13 million in other types (*China Labour Statistical Yearbook 1998*, p. 7).

It is also worthy to note that SOEs have, since the mid-1990s, ceased to be the single most attractive source of employment for university graduates looking for jobs. Alongside with the development of the non-public sector, foreign-funded and private enterprises also became attractive for people seeking employment. According to an investigation conducted in 1998 on the employment preference of university graduates, 40.9 per cent of respondents preferred SOEs, 44.1 per cent chose foreign-funded enterprises, and 15.1 per cent selected private enterprises (Wang, 1999).

Workers began to be employed in the non-public sector in 1984, and they included those working in various joint ventures, foreign-funded enterprises, enterprises funded by residents from Hong Kong, Macao and Taiwan, and shareholding companies. Between 1984 and 1998, as the non-public ownership economy expanded, the number of employees in the non-state sector increased from 0.37 million to 16.28 million (*China Labour Statistical Yearbook 1998*, p. 22; *China Statistical Yearbook 1999*, p. 148) (Table 3.1).

However, the majority of urban employees were still formal employees in state-owned and collectively owned enterprises. At the end of 1998, the percentage of formal employees accounted for about 60 per cent of the urban labour force. Formal employees were further classified into three groups in terms of their employment status: contractual, long-term and temporary employees (*China Statistical Yearbook 1998*, p. 605). For instance, of the 146.68 million formal employees at the end of 1997, there were 77.08 million contractual employees (52.6%), 9.2 million temporary employees (6.3%) and about 60 million other types of long-term employees in various types of enterprises, public institutions and governmental organizations (*China Labour Statistical Yearbook 1998*, pp. 30-32).

Table 3.1: Changes in the situation of urban employees by types of ownership, 1978-98 (million persons)

Year	Total no. of urban employees	In SOEs	In collectively owned enterprises	In enterprises with other types of ownership
1978	95.14	74.51	20.48	–
1979	–	–	–	–
1980	105.25	80.19	24.25	–
1981	–	–		–
1982	–	–	–	–
1983	–	–	–	–
1984	–	–	–	–
1985	128.08	89.90	33.24	0.38
1986	–	–	–	–
1987	137.83	96.54	34.88	0.50
1988	142.67	99.84	35.27	0.63
1989	143.90	101.08	35.02	0.82
1990	166.16	103.46	35.49	8.33
1991	169.77	106.64	36.28	9.74
1992	172.41	108.89	36.21	11.15
1993	175.89	109.20	33.93	16.34
1994	184.13	112.14	32.85	23.07
1995	190.93	112.61	31.47	29.28
1996	198.15	112.44	30.16	32.81
1997	202.07	110.44	28.83	37.62
1998	206.78	90.58	19.63	48.97

Source: 'China Statistical Yearbook 1999', pp. 136-7.
–: Information not available.

It has been mentioned that economic reforms have affected most deeply the livelihood of formal employees in the state-owned and collectively owned enterprises. Indeed, along with the deepening of economic reforms, formal employees have gradually lost their employment security, and they have come to be associated with various economically negative terms as 'surplus employees', 'laid-off formal employees', the unemployed, 'economically constrained employees', etc. And combined with the prolonged poor performance in the state sector, the urban labour force has been shifting rapidly from the public to the non-public economic sector. Particularly since the mid-1990s, continued increases in the number of urban labour force have been paralleled with decreases in the number of formal employees in the public sector. Hence, while the number of urban employees steadily increased during the period from 1995 to 1998, the number of formal employees decreased from 112.61 million to 90.58

million in SOEs.

In sum, reforms in the labour system in China have broken the 'iron rice bowls' for permanent workers and made them less dependent on their enterprises. The traditional employment security for urban employees has thus gradually been removed. But labour mobility across enterprises of different types of ownership is still very much constrained by the fact that social security protection is largely absent in the non-public sector.

Reform of the Wage System

Another component of SOEs reforms was the reform of the wage system. During the planned economy era, the determination of the wage level was highly centralized. While the central government alone designed the wage policies, local governments and enterprises were responsible for implementing them. In general, wages were set by applying unified standards to enterprises all over the country and differences existed across enterprises with different types of ownership.

Within each individual enterprise, wages and benefits for employees were differentiated according to lengths of service and positions held; they were not related with either the performance of individual workers or the economic efficiency of the enterprises. As a result, egalitarian distribution became a conspicuous feature of the enterprises prior to the economic reforms and had been widely criticized for its negative effects on the work morale of the employees. Indeed, economic reforms in the cities had started as a response to the prevailing low-spirit and slackness of employees and the inefficiency of the enterprises.

Early attempts to reform the wage system were closely related to the reform policies of expanding the autonomy of the enterprises and returning profits to them. Between 1978 and 1980, the State Council and concerned government departments issued two documents, 'An Announcement on the Implementation of the Bonus and Piecework System of 1978' and 'Temporary Regulations on Piece-rate Wages in SOEs of 1980', calling for local governments and enterprises to adopt piecework wage and bonus systems. The documents stipulated that no ceiling should be provided for the wages of employees under the piecework system, given that their production quotas were appropriately set. Bonuses should also be provided out of the wage bill, and be debited to the production costs account.

In 1984, the State Council issued 'An Announcement on the Provision of Bonuses in SOEs', which decentralized the administration of bonuses in enterprises. Under the new regulations, the state would specify the percentage of, and the tax rate upon, bonuses delivered to employees, while enterprises were given the autonomy in designing their own bonus schemes. The document also provided that the levels of bonuses should be related to economic efficiency, and no ceiling would be applied to the amount of bonuses in enterprises which fulfilled production quotas and made increases in profits and taxes handed over to the state.

Nation-wide reform of the wage system started in 1985, when the State Council issued 'An Announcement on Reforms of the Wage System in SOEs', which decentralized the administration of wages in enterprises. The document contained three measures in reforming the wage system.

First, enterprises would adopt a different wage system from that of government units and public institutions. For enterprises, the total wages would be related to their economic efficiency. Henceforth, increases in the wages of employees would depend on the economic performance of individual enterprises, and the state would no longer arrange for unified increases or adjustments in the wages of employees in enterprises. Levels of wages were allowed to vary across both enterprises and employees due to differences in economic efficiency and individual performance.

Second, the state would adopt a decentralized system in the administration of wages. Specifically, the state will appraise and assign the total wages and the rates of increase for all enterprises at the provincial and municipal level, including cities with separate planning like Guangzhou, and other ministries under the State Council. Local governments and concerned bureaus would then be responsible for appraising and assigning the total wages and the rates of increase, based upon economic efficiency, for enterprises level by level in accordance with the total wages and the rates of increase assigned by the central government to individual localities or sectors.

Third, enterprises would be given the autonomy in designing their own wage systems according to individual situations, provided that the provision was based on the principle of 'distribution according to contribution'. Since then, the reform of the wage system has been moving along two lines: First, enterprises have been trying various forms in distributing wages. Second, the practice of linking total wages of enterprises with economic efficiency has been applied to increasing numbers of enterprises, with the government making continuous efforts to improve the system.

Reforms of the wage system have, however, not altered the general pattern of wage distribution in China in that types of ownership have remained to be the major factor in accounting for the differences in the average wages of formal employees. From 1985 to 1998, the average annual wages increased from 1,213 yuan to 7,668 yuan for formal employees in the state sector, from 967 yuan to 5,331 yuan for those in collectively owned economic units, and from 1,436 yuan to 8,972 yuan for those in economic units of other types of ownership (*China Statistical Yearbook 1999*, p. 160). In addition, average annual wages of formal employees have, over the years, continued to differentiate across enterprises, public institutions and governmental organizations. In 1998, the average annual wages were 7,405 yuan for formal employees in enterprises, 7,620 yuan for those working in public institutions and 7,740 yuan for employees in governmental organizations (*China Statistical Yearbook 1999*, p. 161).

What one can conclude from the above is that while labour reforms have removed the 'iron rice bowls', reforms of the wage system have altered the uniform wage pattern prevalent during the planned economy era and made it more reflective of the performance of the workers.

4 Challenges to Reform of State-owned Enterprises

Formidable Tasks of Reforming SOEs

Since the beginning of the 1990s, the reform of SOEs has been facing formidable challenges. The **first** challenge is the continued decline in the economic performance of SOEs, particularly since the latter half of 1997. In 1997, SOEs made a total loss of 74.4 billion yuan, an increase of 8.2 per cent over that of 1996 (Zhu, 1999). It was further reported that of the 360,678 SOEs in China in 1997, more that half of them were making a loss (He, 1999). Towards the end of 1998, SOEs in China began to feel the negative effects produced by the Asian financial crisis, which had started a year ago and rocked the economy of most Asian countries. As from 1998, previously losing enterprises were increasing their losses while an increasing number of previously profit-making enterprises were becoming losing ones. This can be observed from the change that while state-owned industrial enterprises made a net profit of about 45.1 billion yuan in 1997, they recorded a net loss of 11.01 billion in the first five months of 1998. Of the 512 national key SOEs, the number of losing SOEs also increased from 39 in 1997 to 191 by March 1998, making a total loss of 9.21 billion yuan.

To rescue SOEs out of economic difficulties and to stimulate growth, the government lowered interest rates seven times between 1996 and the first half of 1999. In so doing, the government intended to achieve two purposes at one measure: to keep down the operational costs of SOEs and to stipulate consumption. For a long time, SOEs had incurred huge debts to the banks and were the biggest debtor to the state. It was estimated that by 1997 the total debts that SOEs owned to banks amounted to over 3,000 billion yuan (Zhu, 1999).

However, while SOEs' debts and costs had effectively been reduced due to lowered interest rates, reductions in the bank savings rate produced only limited impact on stimulating consumption. Despite the fact that prices have been declining since the mid-1997, the general population remained to be unenthusiastic in spending. Private savings continued to increase despite the lowered interest rates. Another measure that the government took to stimulate growth was to expand investment. In 1998, the government made an increase of 17.4 per cent in investment in fixed assets in state-owned economic units, but the effects were negligible. In fact, lowered interest rates and expanding investments have so far succeeded little in solving the problems of SOEs. At best, they served to help SOEs not to lay off too many employees.

The **second** challenge is that, along with the deepening of economic reforms, SOEs have been trapped into a dilemma between fulfilling their social obligations and combating market forces. In most cases, SOEs have been heavily burdened by huge numbers of surplus workers and various social obligations such as delivering pensions for a rapidly increasing number of retirees, paying social insurance contributions, providing welfare services and, more recently, providing for laid-off formal employees. Among the various obligations, the problem of surplus workers has presented itself as most formidable. It was estimated that about 20 to 30 per cent of the employees in SOEs were a surplus (Zhou, 1998; Zhang & Zhou, 1999). This means a total of 10 to 15 million workers, out of the 52.2 million formal employees employed by SOEs at the end of 1998.

As mentioned before, SOEs are constrained in dismissing their surplus employees, for both political and economical reasons. Politically, it is because laid-off employees could easily become a source of social instability and SOEs have traditionally been held responsible for maintaining social stability. SOEs must therefore be very cautious in dismissing their surplus workers and, in most situations, they often have to keep as many of them as possible. However, economically, in order to survive in the market, SOEs are pressed to increase their efficiency through reducing the number of employees, and this is also what has been encouraged by the government. So far as the burden on SOEs is concerned, the effect of cutting the number of surplus employees has so far not been significant. Since the early 1990s, surplus employees have been dealt with in the form of laid-off formal employees, and SOEs are required to establish re-employment centres to take care of them, at least on a temporary basis. At the end of September 1998, the number of laid-off formal employees in SOEs reached over 10 million, of which over 7 million were provided for in the 124,000 re-employment service centers established in SOEs (Qiao, 1999). According to governmental regulations, SOEs must provide one-third of the living allowances for laid-off formal employees registered in the re-employment centres.

Other than keeping the surplus workers, the provision of retirement pensions is another burden of SOEs, particularly since the mid-1990s when SOEs began to experience a rapid increase in the number of retirees. As indicated previously, from 1995 to 1998, the number of formal employees in the state-owned economic sector decreased from 109.55 million to 88.09 million (*China Statistical Yearbook 1999*, p. 144). However, from 1980 to 1998, the number of retirees increased from 6.38 million to 27.83 million, with pension payments rising from 4.34 billion yuan to 172.6 billion yuan (*China Statistical Yearbook 1999*, p. 764). In 1997, SOEs had 73.31 million formal employees (*China Labour Statistical Yearbook 1998*, p. 239) and 19.08 million retirees, spending a total of 116.07 billion yuan on pensions plus other welfare payments, equivalent to about 25 per cent of the total wage delivered by SOEs (*China Statistical Yearbook 1999*, p. 241). In 1997, the national average ratio of retirees and formal employees in SOEs was 1 : 3.84 (Zhou, 1998). In some old industries such as textiles, coal and railways, retirement pensions in SOEs sometimes amounted to over 50 per cent of the total wage bill.

Since the early 1990s, along with the implementation of various social insurance programmes, enterprise contributions have proved to be a heavy burden for SOEs. As of 1998, enterprises generally contributed around 20 per cent of the wage bill for pension funds, 6 per cent for medical insurance, 2 per cent for unemployment funds, 0.7-1 per cent for maternity insurance, and 0.5-1.5 per cent for workers' compensation, amounting to over 30 per cent of the wage bill. In some situations, enterprises might have to contribute more than the prescribed rates, particularly for pension funds. For example, in Shanghai, enterprise contribution for pension funds alone amounted to 28 per cent of the wage bill. It was estimated that enterprise contributions might amount to nearly 50 per cent of the wage bill, if housing funds were also included (Zhang & Zhou, 1999).

Finally, enterprise-financed welfare services have continued to be a huge burden for SOEs. As it was a common practice for enterprises to finance welfare services, including medical care, for their employees during the planned economy era, many SOEs have to carry these 'assets' into the reform period. The operation of these welfare services required, nevertheless, substantial financial input by enterprises. In the state-owned economic sector, employee welfare expenditures in 1997 reached 82.06 billion yuan (*China Labour Statistical Yearbook 1998*, p. 505), of which SOEs spent over 54.45 billion yuan, about 12 per cent of the total wages at 472.19 billion yuan. It was estimated that in 1997 various employee welfare facilities accounted for around 15 to 20 per cent of the assets in state-owned industrial enterprises, with welfare expenditure amounting to about 50 per cent of the managerial costs, or about 60 billion yuan (Zhu, 1998).

Largely because of the social obligations of the enterprises, the government has to be very cautious in carrying out the economic reforms, preventing as far as possible the losing enterprises to go bankrupt. One of the methods that had been used in the 1980s was to persuade the profit-making enterprises to take over the losing ones. However, this method had often produced the result of turning profit-making enterprises into losing ones, as the burden that they had to take up was too heavy. Bankruptcy was hence allowed for the losing enterprises since the early 1990s, which made the number of enterprises declaring bankrupt increased to 6,222 in 1996. The number of bankrupt enterprises was in fact rather small when compared with the total number of enterprises. But even with this small number, objection was raised by the banks as the policy was to allow enterprises declaring bankrupt to compensate first their employees and retirees, with little assets left for the banks. As a result, many SOEs, notwithstanding their losses, were allowed to go on operating for fear of causing social instability.

The **third** challenge to SOEs reforms is the difficulty of 'separating government from enterprises', as a clearly defined government-enterprise relationship is still lacking. For most of the time during the reform period, while the efforts of the government had concentrated on separating the government from the enterprises by employing such methods as contracting out, leasing, and forming various forms of stockholding companies, results were far from satisfactory. Evidence showed that the implementation of these responsibility measures was only effective in the early years of reform and their effects tended to be short-run. Furthermore, the ill-defined government-enterprise relationship and the poor managerial skills of the managers had turned many enterprises into red, with some of the managers becoming corrupt themselves.

Obstacles to Reform of SOEs

Since the early 1990s when the goal of economic reforms shifted to the building of modern enterprises, stockholding companies have become the synonym of modern enterprises, with most large and medium-size state and collectively owned enterprises transformed into various forms of stockholding entities, with boards of directors, supervisors' and employees' representative meetings established within the enterprises. Under these arrangements, enterprises were given the autonomy in production and management and were held responsible for profits and losses, but the tradition of the planned economy had proved to be too tenacious to break. In brief, although enterprise autonomy and responsibility had been expanded and defined more clearly by laws and regulations, the ambiguous relationship between the government and SOEs remained.

For example, within each SOE, and collectively owned enterprises as well, relevant government bureaus possessed still the power to set up administrative agencies, with the responsibility to appoint managers or contractors. This situation certainly denied enterprises the full autonomy to monitor their performance. In fact, for most of the managers, they would not lose anything should their enterprises go bankrupt, nor would they gain anything if profits were made. In other words, the real boss of the SOEs continued to be the state and there was no wonder that many managers had hardly any incentive to make profits. Short-term practices and corruption remained a common feature of the SOEs, particularly among managers approaching retirement age. This has led to the debate about whether poor performance in SOEs is the result of human or system influences (He, 1999). The establishment of the special team of inspectors, put directly under the State Council in 1998, seems to suggest that the failure of the SOEs to reform themselves is largely the result of human greediness.

The ambiguous relationship between SOEs and the government has further contributed to the prolonged decline in the economic performance of the SOEs. Although enterprises were legally defined as independent economic entities by the Enterprise Law and given autonomy in production and management, SOEs had so far not attained this status. On the one hand, SOEs had continued to perform many governmental responsibilities in that various grass-roots structures of the party, government and social organizations were still established within SOEs. At the end of 1997, over 20 per cent of employees in SOEs were taken up by such positions (Zhang & Zhou, 1999). Such a large percent of non-production personnel had not only raised the operational costs, but also had negatively affected the efficiency of SOEs. It is indeed unacceptable for modern enterprises to be interfered in this way by the government machinery. On the other hand, while various governmental bureaus were playing an active role in managing the operation of SOEs, none of them was responsible for the latter's performance. In other words, although SOEs reforms in China started with expanding the autonomy of the enterprises, SOEs had never gained their full independence.

Finally, there is the belief that current difficulties in SOEs reforms are the result of conflicting interests. It was said that relating parties like government officials, banks, and even managers and employees of SOEs themselves were in fact not motivated to support reforms of the SOEs because their interests would negatively be affected (Wang, 1999). So far, government officials had been playing an active role not only on the political stage, but also in the economic arena as they actually controlled the operation of the SOEs. If SOEs were reformed into truly modern enterprises with autonomy of their own, many government officials would lose their grounds to play a part in the economy and some of them would even become jobless themselves.

Being quasi-governmental and monopoly agencies, banks in China had held an advantageous position in their relationship with the SOEs. On the one hand, low interest rates and fund shortages had given the banks, which control the lending of loans, the power to make decisions fatal to the survival of the SOEs. On the other hand, due to various political or personal factors, banks were frequently pressurized to provide loans to SOEs that would result in bad debts. Currently, the average liabilities of SOEs have reached over 75 per cent, with some reaching 95 per cent, and most of the loans have come from banks. Should SOEs reforms lead to bankruptcies or mergers, it would imply huge losses on the part of banks. In fact, the deepening of economic reforms is bound to result in the transformation of governmental banks into commercial banks, forcing them to compete in the market. The monopoly position of the governmental banks would then be removed, and this is certainly not a change that the bank managers would like to see.

For the employees and retirees of SOEs, they would also not welcome too big a change of their rice bowls which they have tried so hard to preserve for so many years. Before the implementation of the reform policies, employees of SOEs constituted the top stratum in the social stratification of China. Traditionally, enterprises in the cities were divided into two types: SOEs and collectively owned enterprises, of which the former had many advantages over the latter. SOEs had also proved to be an important factor in maintaining social stability in the cities, even during such politically turbulent times as the Cultural Revolution period. It was because SOEs and, to a lesser extent, collectively owned enterprises, provided both security and privileges for their employees. Being once a highly privileged class and beneficiaries of the planned economy, employees and retirees of SOEs would of course resist any drastic changes.

In sum, SOEs reforms in China still have a long way to go before accomplishing the goal of turning themselves into modern enterprises. While debates have been going on surrounding such matters as the relationship between ownership and efficiency, there is an increasing recognition that market economy does not fit well with the current political system of China or vice versa. Although there are voices to call for political reforms in line with the economic ones, the government has so far shown little interests in reforms outside of the economic system. In short, the failure of SOEs to transform themselves into modern enterprises reflects, to a large extent, that the government is unprepared to give up its control over the SOEs. The government fears that the full autonomy of the SOEs would ultimately lead to an erosion of the foundation of the socialist system.

PART TWO

FROM LABOUR INSURANCE TO SOCIAL SECURITY

5 Shortcomings of the Labour Insurance Regulations

Introduction

Prior to the economic reforms, employees in the urban areas of China were covered by a single package of labour insurance benefits established in 1951. As this old labour insurance system was financed exclusively by individual enterprises for their own employees, social security in China during the planned economy era was frequently referred to as 'enterprise-financed security'. In fact, employment was the most important source of security for urban residents before the economic reforms because social insurance and welfare benefits were generally unavailable for individuals outside the workplace.

Therefore, social security reforms in China have been moving along two directions since economic reforms started in 1978: One has been to convert enterprise-financed labour insurance into a unified social insurance pooling system with the government, enterprises and individuals sharing in funding. Another has been to expand the coverage of social security to all residents in the urban areas, including those who are not employed by enterprises or other work units. In this sense, while economic reforms have diversified the economy and the labour force, attempts to reform the labour insurance regulations system have been to bring employees belonging to different types of enterprises under a unified system.

China has implemented, in the last decade, a series of regulations and laws aimed at establishing, what the government described 'a socialist social security system with Chinese characteristics'. While the old labour insurance system has not totally been dismantled, it is now replaced by a number of separate schemes including old-age pensions, unemployment insurance, workers' compensation, and maternity insurance.

The Three-tier Protection for the Urban Unemployed

Mention should first be made of the changes in provision for the unemployed, as the labour insurance regulations were totally unprepared to tackle the problem of unemployment, a phenomenon unheard of before the economic reforms. While the development of unemployment insurance will be a subject of discussion in the next chapter, it suffices to point out here that for the urban employees, particularly those working in SOEs, the new social security system now consists of a three-tier safety net.

The first tier is provided for the laid-off formal employees in SOEs, which is, as explained later, a special form of unemployment benefit in China. The benefit for laid-off formal employees is jointly financed by enterprises, the government and the unemployment insurance funds on a one-third-for-each basis, and is administered by re-employment service centres established by enterprises to deal with laid-off formal employees. Employees displaced by enterprises are first provided for in these centres, where they can receive financial assistance and employment services for a maximum period of three years.

The second tier of safety net is the unemployment insurance. If a laid-off formal employee fails to find a job within three years in the re-employment centres, he or she will become an unemployed person in status, and will be eligible for unemployment benefits for a maximum of 24 months.

The third tier of the safety net is the poverty relief programme, which is administered by the Ministry of Civil Affairs and provides social relief in cash to individuals and families whose per capita family income is below the locally determined poverty line. Both the government and the work units would join hands in financing the social relief programme in the cities. However, if funds were not available from the work units, the government would then have to shoulder the entire responsibility. Laid-off formal employees and the unemployed living on benefits are also eligible for poverty relief if their per capita family income is below the set standards.

Other than unemployment, the old labour insurance regulations have also been found to be incapable of tackling other problems that have emerged as a result of the economic reforms. What are the problems that have emerged? What are the shortcomings of the traditional labour insurance regulations? What measures that the Chinese government has taken in meeting the new needs for social security protection? These are the questions that will be explored below.

Reform of the Traditional Labour Insurance System

The first nation-wide unified formal social insurance system was established in China in 1951 through the implementation of the State Council's 'Regulations on Labour Insurance', which applied to SOEs, government units, public institutions and mass organizations all over China. This system covered all the benefits for employees, including pensions, medical care, workers' compensation, maternity benefits, and other temporary relief programmes. Large collectively owned enterprises also followed the same rules as were recommended by the government.

Although the labour insurance regulations subsequently underwent several changes, three prominent features remained unchanged throughout the pre-reform period: First, benefits were provided to cover the needs of employees and their family members 'from cradle to grave', and increased in amount along with the economic growth. Second, individual contributions were not required, and funds came from planned allocations by the state. Third, except pensions for the retired, other provisions under the labour insurance regulations remained largely unchanged during the pre-reform period. The following discussion on the reform of the traditional labour insurance system will thus focus on the old-age pensions for retired employees.

The initial system under the regulations of 1951 applied to three sectors; (1) the railway and shipping sector; (2) posts and telecommunications; and (3) enterprises with more than 100 employees. The system was funded exclusively by contributions from participating enterprises. As both the number and proportion of enterprise retirees were small at that time, a contribution rate of 3 per cent of the wage bill was more than sufficient to finance the system on a largely pay-as-you-go basis. Seventy per cent of the funds were retained locally to pay the necessary pensions while 30 per cent were transferred to a national master fund as reserves for adjustment purposes. The All-China Federation of Trade Unions managed both local payments and the master fund. Retirement ages were set at 60 for men and 55 for women, with additional adjustments for hazardous jobs. Employees were allowed to retire after 25 years of service (20 years for women), of which 10 years had to be spent in the enterprise from where the worker retired. Old-age pensions usually covered 35-60 per cent of the standard wage.

In the following years, the coverage of the system was expanded and benefits were raised. The 'Resolution on Several Revisions of the Regulations on Labour Insurance' passed in January 1953 extended the coverage to include SOEs with fewer than 100 employees; the requirement for 10 years of service in the enterprise from where the worker retired was reduced to 5 years; and pension benefits were raised from 35-60 per cent of the wage to 50-70 per cent. To simplify the calculation of benefits, the All-China Federation of Trade Unions stipulated in 1954 that the 'standard wage' would be used as the basis for calculating pension benefits for all retired employees.

The 'Temporary Regulations on the Retirement of Employees in Government' passed in 1955 established a separate system for employees in governmental organs and public institutions, with retirement benefits covering 50-80 per cent of the wage. To avoid conflicts arising from different treatment of employees from enterprises and governmental organs by the two separate retirement schemes, the 'Temporary Regulations on the Retirement of Employees and Staff' enacted in 1958 combined the two schemes into a single one, applicable to both enterprise and government employees. Pension benefits covered 50-70 per cent of the standard wage for both types of employees. This arrangement operated until it was halted during the Cultural Revolution period (1966-1976) when the All-China Federation of Trade Unions and the Ministry of Labour were abolished. Responsibility for pension provision and administration was then directly transferred to enterprises, with local labour departments taking up the supervisory role. This change began the era of 'enterprises managing the society (welfare)' or 'enterprise insurance'.

When economic reforms started in 1978, the State Council issued two new regulations (Document 104), dividing the pension system of 1958 again into two separate schemes. 'Temporary Regulations on the Retirement and Resignation of Employees' applied to employees in enterprises, and 'Temporary Regulations on the Arrangements for Old, Weak, Sick and Disabled Cadres' was designed for employees of governmental organizations. One reason for the division of the system into two separate schemes was the concern for providing special arrangements for the retirement of old revolutionary cadres. Retirement ages were reaffirmed at 60 for men and 50 for women (55 for female cadres), while qualifications were further eased and benefits raised under both schemes. Both types of employees were allowed to retire after 10 years of continuous service. Benefits were related to the length of service years and the final standard wage. For normal retirees, that is, workers who had worked for 20 continuous years would receive a monthly pension of 75 per cent of the standard wage; those who had worked for 15 to 20 continuous years would get 70 per cent; and those with 10 to 15 years of service could get 60 per cent.

In addition, a minimum monthly pension of 25 yuan was guaranteed. Disability pensions were raised from 60-75 per cent to 80-90 per cent of the standard wage according to the extent of care needed, with a minimum guaranteed pension of 35 yuan per month. The former lump-sum payment for employees who resigned from work changed to a monthly pension of 40 per cent of the standard wage, with a minimum guaranteed pension of 20 yuan per month. For employees of governmental organs and public institutions, a privileged retirement scheme was designed specially for certain groups of old cadres whose service years went back before the founding of the PRC. Retired cadres covered under this special arrangement could receive a monthly pension equivalent to 80-100 per cent of the standard wage. Large, municipal collectively owned enterprises were required to follow the same rules while small or district collectively owned enterprises were allowed to design their own plans according to individual situations.

Problems of the Old-age Pension System

The basic rules contained in the State Council's Document 104 of 1978 have continued into the 1990s, serving as the blueprint for handling retirement of employees in both urban enterprises and governmental organs. But the substance of the provisions had many times been revised in the course of implementation that the labour insurance regulations, even before the start of the economic reforms, could hardly be said to have reflected the 'socialist superiority'.

One dilemma that the government had to face, as it began to reform the labour insurance regulations, was to contain the overall costs, especially in pension payments, and at the same time to increase benefits for a rapidly increasing number of retirees. Generous retirement benefits and easier qualifications under the regulations of 1978 provided incentives for employees to retire early, which was also explicitly encouraged by the government in order to create jobs for the large number of workers returning to the cities after the Cultural Revolution. The number of retirees increased fivefold between 1978 and 1985, and overall pension costs rose from 2.8 per cent of total wages for urban employees to 10.6 per cent (World Bank, 1997). Government and enterprises alike have since been over-burdened by the huge outlay on old-age pension obligations accumulated over the years.

Another problem was that since SOEs reforms started in the early part of the 1980s, the wage structure for both the private and the public sectors had been transformed, which made the pensions appear increasingly inadequate. Bonuses and various subsidies had been increased so much in the first few years of wage restructuring that for some workers, they might represent as large a sum as the wage itself. Since pensions were linked to the final standard wage, excluding bonuses and subsidies, the amount of pensions actually received by the retirees might therefore be a much smaller sum of what the workers used to earn before retirement. With soaring inflation in the 1980s, inadequate retirement benefits often became a source of social unrest.

To ease the anger of the retirees, pension reforms during the 1980s were characterized by tireless efforts of the government to make adjustments in the level of pension benefits so as to reduce the gap in incomes between employees and the retirees. In 1983, the minimum guaranteed pension was raised from 25 yuan to 30 yuan per month for normal retirees, from 35 yuan to 40 yuan per month for disabled retirees, and from 20 to 25 yuan for employees who resigned from their posts. The privileged retirement system was extended to include all cadres who started working before the founding of the PRC, and was also made applicable to enterprise employees who had the same qualifications. In 1989, a general increase was made in retirement benefits in line with the wage increase for employees of SOEs. At the same time, the minimum guaranteed pension increased from 30 to 50 yuan for normal retirees, from 40 to 60 yuan for disabled retirees, and from 25 to 40 yuan for employees who resigned from their posts. In 1992, another 10 per cent general increase was made in retirement benefits, with a minimum guaranteed increase of 10 yuan for each retiree. In addition, in order to cushion the effects of inflation on the living standards of the retirees, the State Council made five increases, from 1985 to 1995, in the retirement benefits either through providing additional subsidies or by raising directly the benefit levels.

The traditional old-age pension system, as described above, was undoubtedly the product of the centrally planned economy era, and was a largely urban-based, pay-as-you-go and defined benefit type that covered mainly urban employees working in the state sector. Problems such as partial coverage and limited pooling increasingly presented themselves as the major obstacles to the economic reforms that started in the urban areas since the mid-1980s. The shortcomings of the old system were so obvious that in 1985 the Chinese leaders decided to do something about it.

First, the Chinese leaders recognized that in order that China might survive the threat of population aging in the not too distant future, the establishment of a new pension system covering the entire population was the only way out. Partial coverage, as was the case with the traditional system, would leave a majority of the future elderly people in China without any protection when they retired from work.

Second, partial coverage would also impede labour mobility, particularly for employees to move from the state to the non-state sector, which was seen as a key factor in the establishment of a socialist market economy and for China to restructure its SOEs. As social benefits in China, such as old-age pensions and other welfare services under the traditional labour insurance regulations, were mainly confined to those employed in the state sector, SOEs employees must think twice before contemplating leaving their present positions. Furthermore, since

Finally, the old method of providing benefits had also been widely criticized for being neither adequate nor just because it did not consider inflation and benefits were not related to contributions.

Immediately following the establishment of social pooling around 1992, local governments began to turn their attention to reforming the methods of providing benefits. The common objective of the reform was to make benefits more closely related to individual contributions, and two different methods were proposed for adoption to achieve this purpose. One was to base benefits on individual contributions, and the other on entitlements accumulated during the employment years. In 1992, the Ministry of Labour drafted a proposal for reforming the method of pension provision, inviting suggestions from localities. After conducting experiments in more than one hundred cities or counties, the Ministry issued in October 1993 'An Announcement for Experiments on Reforming the Methods of Providing the Basic Pension Benefit', recommending local governments to implement the following reform policies:

1. The financing of the basic benefit should be shared between the state, enterprises and individual employees. Enterprises contribute a certain percentage of the wage bill as decided by local governments, and individuals contribute 2 per cent of the wage. Wages in excess of 200 per cent of the monthly average local wage should not be included in the earnings base used for calculating individual contributions. Employees with wages 60 per cent below the average local wage contribute 60 per cent of the average local wage.
2. The basic benefit consists of a social pension and a premium pension. The wage base used for calculating the social pension is the average local wage, and benefits are provided based on number of individual contribution years. A worker who has contributed for over 15 years or above gets 25 per cent of the average local wage; a worker who has contributed for 10 to 15 years gets 20 per cent of the average wage; and a worker with 5 to 10 years receives 15 per cent. The wage base used for calculating the premium pension is the worker's indexed average monthly wage during the contribution years. Benefits are provided based on both the indexed average wage and the number of years of individual contribution. A worker who has contributed for 5 years and above gets 1 per cent of the indexed average monthly wage for each contribution year; a worker who has contributed for less than 5 years receives a lump-sum payment equivalent to 3 months' indexed average wage for each year of contribution.
3. If the application of the new method results in a decrease in the basic benefit for retirees, as compared with the benefit provided under the

old method, the differences will be covered from the pool. If the new method results in an increase in the benefit, the increase should be contained under 20 per cent.

4. An adjustment mechanism should be established to index the basic benefit to increases in the wages of current employees. An adjustment in line with increases in the average local wage should be made on next July 1, following the retirement of the worker. Employees who retired before the application of this method should continue with the old arrangements, and their basic benefit can be adjusted by applying this method.

As a result of the above announcement, the basic tier of benefits was now related to both the lengths of service and individual contributions. The social pension was provided based on the length of contribution years and the average local wage, reflecting the principle of social equity; while the premium pension was based on the indexed average wage of the retiree during his or her employment years, reflecting the principle of efficiency.

The State Council Document 6 of 1995

Document 33 of 1991 applied mainly to SOEs, and collectively owned enterprises were allowed to design their own pension schemes with reference to the regulations. In the following years, the coverage of the pension system generally expanded. Between 1990 and 1996, the number of covered formal employees and retirees increased from 52 million and 9.65 million to 87.58 million and 23.58 million respectively (*China Social Security 1997*, no. 10, p. 15). However, participants still came mainly from the state sector. Employees in most collectively owned enterprises and enterprises with other types of ownership were generally left out of the coverage. Among the 87.58 million covered formal employees by the end of 1996, 70.45 million (80%) were employees of the SOEs, while 14.55 million (16.61%) were employees of collectively owned enterprises and 2.58 million (2.95%) were employees of enterprises with other types of ownership.

Overall, in 1991, the pension plan covered 78.4 per cent of the formal employees employed in various types of enterprises. Nevertheless, the coverage was extremely uneven across enterprises: 95.15 per cent for SOEs, 51.47 per cent for collectively owned enterprises, and 27.48 per cent for enterprises with other types of ownership. With over 20 per cent of the formal employees being left out of the coverage, the pension burdens of SOEs remained unsolved. Furthermore, pension burdens were also spread unevenly across sectors, localities and individual enterprises. Across the various industrial sectors, the pension burden coefficient ranged from 0.375 (each contributor supporting 0.375 pensioner) for the non-ferrous metal industry to 0.058 for civil aviation; across localities, the coefficient ranged from 0.472 for Shanghai to 0.192 for Shandong. As for the contribution rates, while the average was about 20 per cent of the total wage bill, some enterprises paid over 30 per cent. The differences in contributions also varied greatly between the participating and the non-participating enterprises as the latter were usually those with few or no retirees (Hu, 1998).

In view of the above problems, the State Council issued another document, Document 6, in 1995 spelling out two major themes: One was to expand the pension coverage and the other was to lay down the financial principles regarding social pooling and individual accounts. The above two themes were set in adherence to the "Decisions on the Establishment of Socialist Market Economy' passed by the Third Plenary Session of the Fourteenth Central Committee Meeting held in 1993. The basic message of the principles was that the new system must reflect both social equity and efficiency and put together the spirits of mutual support and self-protection. State Council Document 6 of 1995 set forth the following broad guidelines for pension reforms:

1. The goals of the current pension reform are defined as the establishment of a unified pension system for all types of enterprises and employees in both urban and rural areas by the turn of this century. The system will have multiple channels of funding and multiple tiers of benefits, and will combine the social and the individual accounts. It will take into consideration both the rights and obligations of individual employees, and its management will be socialized. In addition, 'four-unification' in the basic tier of benefits will gradually be put in place and they are: (1) equal treatment for all types of enterprises and employees by a unified system; (2) unified standards for contributions and benefits; (3) unified management; and (4) unified use of adjustment funds.
2. The principles of enterprise pension reforms are that benefit standards should match the levels of economic growth and the affordability of the involved parties, interweave mutual support and self-protection, and take into consideration both equity and efficiency. Management should be conducted according to the appropriate rules and must follow the above unification policies, and administration of the schemes should be separated from fund management.

3. Third, the basic tier should be funded jointly by enterprises and individual employees. Individual contributions should gradually be increased along with that in the wages of the employees.
4. Finally, the document requires 80 per cent of the pension fund balances be invested in government bonds after a sufficient sum is retained for two months' retirement payments.

Furthermore, Document 6 of 1995 also put up two options for local governments to adopt in relation to the basic tier, in which social pooling and individual accounts were combined in varying degrees.

Option One placed greater emphases on individual accounts, with enterprises contributing 8 per cent of each worker's total wage and 5 per cent of the average local wage, while individuals contributing 3 per cent of their own wage, making approximately 16 per cent in total. Over time, it was hoped that contributions from enterprises would decrease and individual contributions would increase until individuals were contributing about half of the total to their own accounts. Thus, when a worker reached retirement age and had contributed for at least 15 years, he or she would then be entitled to a monthly pension, equivalent to 1/120 of the fund accumulated in the individual account. As individual accounts applied only to new employees who joined after the implementation of the plan, those who had already retired and current employees not fully covered by individual accounts would continue with the old arrangements, with their benefits adjusted annually and provided out of the social pool.

Option Two emphasized more on social pooling than the use of individual accounts. For those whose contribution years exceeded 10 years, benefits would consist of a social pension equivalent to 20-25 per cent of the average local wage, and a premium pension equivalent to 1.0-1.4 per cent of their own average wage for each year of contribution. Further, an individual account pension could be drawn as a lump sum or in the form of an annuity.

The direction of pension reforms as stipulated in Document 6 of 1995 was to make a transition from the then pay-as-you-go system to a partially-funded system, consisting of both social pooling and individual accounts. By the end of 1996, most localities had established the system of social pooling plus individual accounts, covering over 42 million formal employees. However, the implementation of Document 6 had also resulted in some unexpected consequences.

First, as Document 6 allowed local governments to choose among the two proposed options or invent their own schemes according to individual local situations, a variety of local designs were developed across the country, varying widely in design, administration and benefit levels. Such a varied pension system was not only contrary to the intention of the central government for unification; it also posed problems such as portability and variations in benefit levels across localities. Furthermore, it also impeded the establishment of a nationally unified labour market, which was one of the major objectives that pension reforms had aimed to achieve.

Second, as most local schemes were operated at either the district or the county level, separate plans were maintained for different enterprises and for employees with different types of ownership. With limited funding base, these schemes were also extremely constrained in guaranteeing timely payment of benefits.

Third, to enable enterprises in the localities to compete in the market, local governments tended to raise benefits for the employees or reduce their contribution rates. In 1995, the actual rates of employee contribution in most localities were around 2 per cent of the wages, lower than the officially stipulated 3 to 4 per cent, while benefits often reached over 80 per cent of the wages (*China Labour and Social Security Ministry, 1999a*, p. 178).

Fourth, individual accounts that had been set up were generally notional, meaning that fully funded accounts were either regarded as unnecessary or unaffordable by local governments. As a result, most of the pension schemes in the localities continued to operate on a pay-as-you-go basis.

Finally, due to loopholes in funds management, reports were not infrequent that pension funds had been misused or diverted by local governments for other purposes, resulting in huge losses to the funds (*China Labour and Social Security Ministry, 1999a*).

The State Council Document 26 of 1997

With the economic reforms focussing, since the mid-1990s, on the establishment of modern enterprises, restructuring of state assets through the market became the dominant theme in SOEs reforms. Closures, mergers, change of production line, or bankruptcy were threatening the SOEs. As more and more enterprises were laying off their employees, and an increasing number of enterprises delaying, reducing or simply ceasing to pay wages or pensions, workers became more and more uncertain about their employment, incomes and entitlements. Insecurity prevailed as a result among the general population. Under these conditions, the establishment of an adequate social security system was generally viewed as a paramount and urgent task for the government.

It was perceived in the mid-1990s that a sound social security system was not only helpful in the maintenance of social stability, but also necessary for the revival of the labour market, upon which further reforms of SOEs depended. Meanwhile, the pension system that came out of the 1995 State Council Document, as discussed above, was widely regarded as incapable of combating the nation-wide insecurity; in fact, the new pension system has imposed additional constraints upon the deepening of economic reforms.

In July 1997, the State Council issued another document, Document 26, on the reform of the pension system. The document contained two major objectives: One was to improve the function of the then pension system through correcting the defects that had surfaced so far, and the other was to make the pension system more conducive to economic reforms. Document 26 re-emphasized the objectives of pension reforms as were outlined in Document 6 of 1995. In proposing the establishment of a unified system for the basic tier, Document 26 stipulated that local governments must implement the following 'four-unification' by the end of 1998:

1. A unified pension system should be applied to all enterprises and employees with all types of ownership.
2. Contribution rates are to be unified, with 20 per cent of the wage bill as the ceiling for contribution by enterprises, and a minimum of 4 per cent of the wage for individual employees. Starting from 1998, individual contributions will be raised by 1 per cent every two years until individual employees are contributing 8 per cent of their wage.
3. Contributions to individual accounts will be unified at a total of 11 per cent of a worker's wage. With the individual contribution rate gradually increasing to 8 per cent over time, enterprises will eventually be contributing 3 per cent.
4. The method of providing benefits is to be unified. Basic benefits will consist of a basic pension and an individual account pension. A worker who reaches retirement age after contributing for at least 15 years gets a monthly basic pension equivalent to 20 per cent of the average local wage in the year prior to retirement, and a monthly individual account pension equivalent to the funds accumulated in the individual account divided by 120. Those who have already retired shall continue with the old arrangements, and current employees who began work before the unification of the basic tier should gradually be brought under the coverage of the new scheme through combining the methods of both the old and the new.

To make the new pension system more viable, Document 26 substantially redistributed pension burdens across enterprises, reduced the replacement rates of benefits, decreased the contribution rates by enterprises, and increased that for employees. Previously, in many localities, enterprise contributions were based on the sum of pensions payable plus a certain percentage of the wage bill. Pension burdens were thus particularly heavy on enterprises with more retirees. By changing the base for enterprises to make contributions to a certain percentage of the wage bill alone, Document 26 effectively reduced the contributions of enterprises with more retirees while that for enterprises with few or no retirees would be increased. The new method of providing benefits also reduced the replacement rate of benefits from over 80 per cent to below 60 per cent, in accordance with the principle that benefit levels should be affordable by the economy. Finally, the new regulations reduced the contributions by enterprises and increased that for individual employees.

Following the implementation of Document 26 of 1997, in August 1998, the State Council issued 'An Announcement on Establishing a Unified Pension Plan at the Provincial Level and Transferring Sector Pools to Local Administration'. A provincially unified pension system had, in fact, been promoted by the central government since the early 1990s. By the end of 1997, however, there were altogether only 13 provincial localities (including provinces, cities directly under the central government and provincial autonomic districts) had established unified social pooling at the provincial level. Among them, only Beijing, Shanghai and Tianjin applied unified management and standards to their systems. In other localities, provincial pooling was largely nominal, having either difficulty in unifying the contribution rates and benefits or in collecting provincial adjustment funds. As separate pension schemes had already been operating in individual localities for more than 10 years, their unification into a provincially unified system involving substantial redistribution of benefits would inevitably invite resistance. To facilitate a smooth change in the local systems, the 1998 Announcement allowed local governments to first establish a provincially unified adjustment mechanism and then a provincially unified pension system by the end of 1998. In early 1999, it was reported that 28 localities (including provinces, provincial autonomous districts and cities directly under the central government) had designed and taken steps to implement a provincially unified pension system (China Labour and Social Security Ministry, 1999a).

As for the sector pools that were created since the mid-1980s for 11 national monopoly sectors, such as railways, banks and civil aviation, changes were less resisted. At the end of 1997, the sector pools covered 19.93 million employees and 4.21 million retirees. Although each sector pool had its own contribution and benefit rates, unification often resulted, however, in improvement for all. Second, as most of these sector pools had been in existence for over 10 years, some had already either restructured or combined with other sectors or simply disappeared. Therefore, the State Council Announcement provided an opportunity for sector pools to reorganize themselves and, with the help of the newly created Ministry of Labour and Social Security, join with the local pools.

Achievements of the Pension Reforms

Pension reforms in China started with three major objectives, one long-term and two short-term. The long-term objective was to deal with the income security of a rapidly aging population, which was projected to reach its heights around the middle of the twenty-first century. The two short-term or more urgent ones were to relieve SOEs of the pension burdens inherited from the planned economy era and to facilitate the development of the labour market in the service of the ongoing economic reforms. Since the implementation of the State Council Document 33 of 1991, which set forth the basic principles and objectives for pension reforms, the reform of the old-age pension system has been moving along a winding path. In the whole 1990s, efforts of the government have been to tinker with the economic system. However, the problems of limited coverage, declining compliance rates and irregular behaviour in funds management presented themselves as three of the obstacles for further reforms.

Limited coverage is the fundamental problem with the existing pension system in China. Pension reforms since the 1990s have been constrained within enterprises with public ownership. At the end of 1998, the pension system covered 84.76 million formal employees in enterprises and 27.27 million retirees. Compared with the 206.78 million urban employees by the end of 1998, the pension system in China covered only 41 per cent of the active urban labour force. Table 4 sets out the situation of pension reforms in China since 1990.

Table 6.1: Situation of pension reforms in China since 1990
(million persons)

Year	Urban employees	Formal employees	Covered enterprise employees	Covered enterprise retirees
1990	166.16	140.59	52.01	9.65
1991	169.77	145.08	–	–
1992	172.41	147.92	–	–
1993	175.89	148.49	73.36	16.28
1994	184.13	148.49	84.94	20.80
1995	190.93	149.08	87.38	22.41
1996	198.15	148.45	87.58	23.58
1997	202.07	146.68	72.78	21.12
1998	206.78	123.37	84.76	27.27

Sources: 'China Statistical Yearbook 1999', p. 136, for urban employees; p. 140, for formal employees; 'China Social Insurance', various years, for covered employees and retirees.
–: Information not available.

In terms of enterprises with different types of ownership, of the 84.76 million covered formal employees by the end of 1998, 67 million (79%) were employees of SOEs, 13.56 million (16%) were from collectively owned enterprises, and 4.24 million (5%) from enterprises with other types of ownership. As for the 27.27 million covered retirees, 21.54 million (79%) retired from SOEs, 5.18 million (19%) from collectively owned enterprises, and 0.55 million (2%) from enterprises with other types of ownership.

The above picture shows that the pension system in China has so far covered mainly formal employees in enterprises with public ownership. Along with the continued shrinkage of the public sector economy and decreases in the number of formal employees, urban employees have been shifting increasingly from the public to the non-public sector. In other words, new urban employees were mostly working in other types of ownership or in private enterprises, rather than being formal employees in the public sector. Therefore, although the pension coverage expanded from 78.4 per cent of enterprise formal employees in 1996 to 96.6 per cent in 1998, the funding base had not undergone significant expansion. The increase in the coverage was mainly due to the fact that the total number of formal employees in enterprises declined abruptly from 111.71 million in 1996 to 86.12 million in 1998 (*China Statistical Yearbook 1999*, p.142).

Because of the partial coverage, the pension system in China is far from being able to provide income security for an aging population as a substantial portion of the urban labour force is still left uncovered. For the same reason, the system also fails to effectively relieve SOEs of the pension burdens, as it is unable to spread the pension burdens across a larger funding base. In fact, the funding base has been shrinking relative to increases in the number of pensioners, resulting in an increase in the pension burdens of the public sector. It can be seen from the figures that between 1993 and 1996, while the number of covered formal employees in enterprises increased from 73.56 million to 87.58 million, covered retirees rose faster from 16.28 million to 23.58 million. Hence, despite the fact that pension funds recorded an increase during the whole 1990s, it can be predicted that in the long run, pension payments will exceed the contributions collected, if nothing is done to the limited and partial coverage.

There is no doubt that a unified pension system that can cover all types of urban employees is what the central government has been promoting since the early 1990s. This was the theme contained in both the State Council's Document 6 of 1995 and Document 26 of 1997. In 1995, the Ministry of Labour designed a 'universal coverage plan', based on the objectives contained in Document 6 of 1995, which were summarized as 'universal coverage with four-unification'. The 'universal coverage plan' was scheduled to extend the coverage, by the end of 1999, to all types of urban employees with unified standards and management. However, it has been found that it was not a simple matter for the existing pension system to extend its coverage to employees in the non-state sector, particularly those working in private enterprises and the self-employed commercial and industrial households. Main difficulties were found to include: (1) 'Informal' employees were widely scattered and pension schemes provided for them were not easy to administer; (2) they frequently changed jobs or became unemployed and pension administrators had difficulties in tracking them and their employers; (3) they usually had unstable or irregular income; and (4) They were suspicious of the promise that they would be given their pensions when they retired, and they tried every means to avoid paying contributions. For the above reasons, the inclusion of the labour force outside the public sector within the pension system has so far not met with much success and the workers presently not covered have also reluctance to join (Hu, 1998).

The second problem is with the compliance rate that has been declining since the mid-1990s. Across the nation, the average compliance rate was 90 per cent in 1997. It declined to 82.7 per cent during the first half of 1998, with 17 localities (referring to provinces, provincial autonomous districts, or cities directly under the central government) having payments exceeding incomes. In September 1998, the compliance rate declined further to 77 per cent, and 25 localities were unable to balance their pension funds. Due to the declining compliance rate, an increasing number of enterprises failed to deliver pensions for their retirees on a timely basis. In 1997, the amount of pensions that enterprises failed to deliver to their pensioners amounted to 3.75 billion yuan, and 2.41 million retirees were affected. By the end of May 1998, the amount of debts that enterprises owed to their pensioners increased to over 8.7 billion yuan, affecting the livelihood of 3.56 million retirees.

Several factors have caused enterprises to delay making contributions or paying pensions for retirees. Poor performance was undoubtedly the most direct cause that had made many SOEs unable to make contributions. Since the mid-1990s, an increasing number of enterprises were running at a loss, and many of them even had difficulties in delivering wages to their employees, let alone making social insurance contributions. Another factor was related to the administration of the new pension system. Usually it was the central government that had invited concerned departments to design and then to introduce the various social insurance measures. Local labour departments at the different levels of administration were then directed to implement them. However, as there was a lack of the appropriate social insurance laws at the local levels, contributions for the various social insurance programmes became optional choices for the enterprises. Campaigns, persuasions or even personal relations had been used as tactics for funds management agencies to coerce the enterprises to make their contributions. But if enterprises or individuals still refused to co-operate, even after pressure from the labour department officials, there was really nothing further that the funds management agencies could do. It was particularly so with the profit-making enterprises form which the local governments collected their revenues.

There is another technical factor that has caused some enterprises not to make their contributions. In some localities, enterprises were allowed to deduct the portion of the contributions that would be returned to them to pay the pensions to their own pensioners before handing them over to the funds management agencies. This practice was known as 'difference-based allocations', by which enterprises contributed to the pension pools only the amount of contributions that were in excess of their pension costs. If the contributions of an enterprise were less than its pension costs, it did not need to make the contributions at all. Instead, the funds management agency would directly allocate from the pool the amount of money it needed to cover the difference. Although the central government did not approve this method, it was practiced in many localities. As a result, contributions were made by enterprises in the form of net losses or gains depending on the number of pensioners or the actual amount of pensions payable, and enterprises were thus divided into two kinds: those making contributions and those receiving returns. The 'contributing' enterprises were naturally unwilling to give, and they tended to avoid handing over the money to the funds management agencies when their contributions exceeded the pension payments. On the other hand, enterprises entitled to receive returns from the pools tended to delay paying their pensioners, as money might not readily be available from the agencies.

Finally, it was a widely spread phenomenon that pension funds were frequently embezzled, misused or diverted to other purposes by individuals or local governments. In 1998, the Labour and Social Security Ministry, the Audit Department and the Finance Ministry together conducted an investigation into the operation of the pension and unemployment insurance funds between 1986 and 1998. It was found that during the period over 10 billion yuan of social insurance funds had been diverted or misused for other purposes by individuals or local governments. Although about 50 per cent of the funds being misused were retrieved as a result of the investigation, a large amount of the funds were still missing.

In January 1999, the State Council issued 'Temporary Regulations on Collecting Social Insurance Contributions', which legalized the procedures and contributions for social insurance. The regulations improved the function of the pension system in several ways: First, they redefined and extended the coverage of social insurance to include all types of urban employees. Second, they enacted the order that covered enterprises must register with local social insurance agencies and declare their contributions. Third, they unified the procedures governing the payment of social insurance contributions, and the 'difference-based allocation' method was discontinued. Enterprises would have to make contributions in full to the pool before making pension payments. Fourth, they established penalties and legal procedures for enterprises or individuals failing to comply with the regulations.

As a result of the enforcement of the 1999 Temporary Regulations, social insurance became compulsory for both enterprises and individuals. Funds management agencies were also able to place a penalty on managers and enterprises or file a suit against them if they refused to contribute. It was reported that the compliance rate has since then been improved.

7 Unemployment Insurance in a Socialist Market Economy

Major Causes of Unemployment

The term 'unemployment' was not officially used in China until 1994. Unemployment in the sense that workers lost their jobs was a rare phenomenon during the pre-reform period. As a socialist country, China was not ready to admit the existence of unemployment, as it was seen as a symbol of the decadent capitalist system. However, as unemployed workers rapidly increased in number since the economic reforms started in 1978, unemployment was such a glaring economic and social problem that the government could no longer ignore it.

During the planned economy era, China adopted a policy of 'high employment and low wages', accompanied by a permanent labour system in the state sector. Workers were assigned, almost without exception, to enterprises by the state according to plans decided at the central level, and their employment was usually on a permanent basis. Enterprises could neither refuse nor dismiss workers assigned to them, and were also obliged to maintain and provide them with the appropriate benefits during their whole working life, as well as the time after retirement. Under this situation, few employees, once they had been assigned, would have the fear of losing their jobs.

It was known, however, that even during the planned economy era, full employment had never been achieved. Some people were still unemployed and they were referred to as 'young people waiting for employment', since most of them were young people just leaving school and had not been assigned to a work unit. Furthermore, though enterprises could not reject workers assigned to them, it was understood that full employment was only maintained at a high cost, as 'implicit' or hidden unemployment or underemployment was rampant in the SOEs. It was estimated that even in the 1990s, SOEs had in general as high as 30 per cent of their employees being surplus employees (*China Labour and Social Security Ministry, 1999b*, p. 44).

When unemployment began to surface as an accompanying product of the economic reforms in China that started in 1978, the former implicit unemployment or underemployment in the enterprises became explicit. Particularly when efforts were made to empower SOEs to become economic entities independent of the government through the introduction of a series of reform measures, an increasing number of employees in SOEs lost their jobs. Unemployment was then accepted as a phenomenon that would happen when SOEs were given increasing autonomy over production and management, and must be responsible for their profits and losses.

As economic reforms deepened, in order to be efficient and competitive in the market, the problem of overstaffing, inherited from the planned economy era, could no longer be tolerated by both the government and the enterprises. As mentioned before, the reform of SOEs has largely been a process whereby enterprises increased efficiency by decreasing the number of employees. Along with the reform of the labour system in the latter part of the 1980s, various measures had been undertaken by the SOEs to restructure their labour force through such methods as 'optimizing regrouping', and 'assignment of posts through merit-selection', which in essence were measures synonymous to reducing employees. As a result, while certain employees would remain with the enterprises, those who were regrouped out would become surplus employees or 'laid-off formal employees'. In short, economic reforms have removed employment security or the 'iron rice bowls' for urban employees in China.

In mid-1990s, the goal of economic reforms in China was defined as one to establish a socialist market economy, and enterprise reforms have since been focused on the establishment of modern enterprises. To accomplish this goal, SOEs have since then undergone a restructuring process. Losing or inefficient enterprises have been closed down, merged, privatized or made to declare bankrupt, while enterprises with developmental potentials have been reorganized into large corporate entities, or converted into stockholding companies or enterprises in various forms. The restructuring process has inevitably led to enormous increases in the number of laid-off formal employees. Meanwhile, economic performance of SOEs towards the end of the twentieth century has been declining. This further aggravated the situation of unemployment in that, on the one hand, an increasing number of employees were forced to leave their jobs and, on the other, employment opportunities became less readily available. Unemployment has thus become a serious problem as China steps into the new century.

Three Alternative Forms of Unemployment

In summary, unemployment has emerged in China in three alternative forms at different times: surplus employees, laid-off formal employees and the unemployed. In the earlier years of economic reforms, unemployed persons were referred to as surplus employees. Surplus workers began to appear around the mid-1980s. They were workers who were 'regrouped out of their posts' due to restructuring. These workers would not necessarily lose their jobs because they could usually continue to be employed by their enterprises in other positions. The term surplus workers implied therefore a temporary status of being out of work. Enterprises continued to provide for them and were responsible for assigning them to suitable positions. Though enterprises were given increasing autonomy over production and management and were encouraged to take measures to reform the permanent labour system, dismissal of workers was an unfamiliar and unacceptable measure for both enterprises and workers. Enterprises were still expected to keep as many workers as possible.

Starting from the early 1990s, as enterprises were gradually relieved of some of their social obligations, and were not obliged to contain surplus workers for long, an increasing number of SOEs adopted measures such as 'difficulty alleviation and organizational transformation' or 'restructuring and transformation'. It was then legitimate for enterprises to screen out and dismiss surplus workers in order to be efficient. Of course, in enterprises that had either been closed down, merged, made bankrupt, the whole force of employees would lose their jobs.

The term 'laid-off formal employees' began to be used in the mid-1990s to refer to employees who had lost their jobs but their employment relations were still maintained with their enterprises. In a way, 'laid-off formal employees', a term still in use, is probably one that can only be found in China and has unique Chinese characteristics. Under this special arrangement, enterprises would continue to take care of their 'sia jiang' (leaving their positions) workers and were held responsible for providing them with the necessary support for a fixed period, usually three years, in the re-employment service centres set up by the enterprises. If the 'laid-off employees' failed to find a job at the end of the period, they would become the unemployed, and were entitled to unemployment benefits for a maximum period of 24 months. A difference between laid-off formal employees and unemployed workers is that the former have lost their job due to a change from the planned to the market economy while the latter's unemployment is the result of an inability to find a job in the market economy. Classifying in this way, laid-off formal employees are thus not held responsible for their unemployment.

The re-employment service centres, which serve as the second line of the social security net, are established in order to cushion the laid-off formal employees to land on the market economy. As such, the unemployed can be described as the hard-core unemployed. Workers would thus first lose their job as the 'laid-off formal employees', and then become the unemployed. Between 1994 and 1998, the number of unemployed workers in China increased from 4.76 million to 5.71 million, and the unemployment rate grew from 2.8 per cent to 3.1 per cent (*China Statistical Yearbook 1999*, p. 133). While the unemployment rate remained low, the number of laid-off formal employees was by no means modest. In 1997, China's SOEs laid off a total number of 12.74 million formal employees, of which 6.34 million were reported to have not found a job at the end of the year (*China Labour Statistical Yearbook 1998*, p. 432). If one includes these laid-off formal employees as the unemployed, the unemployment rate in China would be much higher.

However, economic reforms are only one of the factors that have caused the rise in unemployment and led to the displacement of formal employees from their enterprises. The over supply of labour and the perennial problem of underdevelopment are the other factors that have increased the unemployment rate in China. It was projected that the urban labour force would be increasing at the rate of about 10 million per year in the coming decade. If one added the 80-150 million rural-urban migrant labourers currently seeking work or working in the cities, there is little likelihood for the unemployment rate to subside in China in the foreseeable future.

Unemployment Insurance and Provisions for Laid-off Formal Employees

Since economic reforms started in 1978, China has taken three steps to develop its unemployment insurance. The first locally based unemployment insurance programme was established in China around 1986, in accordance with the State Council Document 77, which required local governments to set up unemployment insurance in SOEs. Initially, the programme covered only the newly recruited contract workers in SOEs. In the following years, eligibility for benefits was gradually extended, as the second step, to the increasing number of formal employees laid off by their enterprises. In 1993, the State Council issued 'Regulations on Unemployment Insurance for Employees in SOEs' (Document 110), which expanded the scope of unemployed workers in SOEs to include all types of workers who had lost jobs due to various factors, entitling them to unemployment benefits. The third major step was made in January 1999 when the State Council issued 'Regulations on Unemployment Insurance', according to which unemployment insurance was legalized and made compulsory for all enterprises in China.

Document 77 of 1986 contained four regulations to reform the labour system: (1) establishing the contract labour system; (2) abolishing the practice of assigning workers to enterprises by the government and replacing it with recruitment of labour through open competition; (3) giving enterprises the authority to dismiss unsatisfactory employees; (4) setting up unemployment insurance in SOEs. Among the four, 'Temporary Regulations on the Establishment of Unemployment Insurance for Employees in SOEs' stipulated the coverage, the financing and provision of benefits, the eligibility criteria and the period of payments of unemployment insurance.

In the first few years of enactment, the coverage of unemployment insurance was very limited. According to the regulations, intended recipients of unemployment benefits must fall into four types of unemployed workers in SOEs: (1) employees from bankrupt enterprises; (2) workers cut off by insolvent enterprises under rectification; (3) workers who lost jobs upon the termination of labour contracts; and (4) dismissed workers. Participating enterprises were required to contribute 1 per cent of the total standard wage bill. Benefits for the unemployed consisted of regular relief payments, medical fees, deaths' assistance, funeral expenses, and survivors' compensation. Funds accumulated would also pay for pensions to retirees of bankrupt enterprises and for providing training and financial assistance to unemployed workers to start small businesses. Both the duration and level of benefits were calculated based on the length of service and the standard wage. The maximum period for an unemployed worker to live on unemployment benefit was 24 months if he or she had over 5 years of service, or 12 months if less than 5 years of service. An unemployed worker could get 60-75 per cent of the standard wage during the first 12 months of unemployment and 50 per cent for the remaining 12 months. The regulations also made it clear that the government would be the ultimate bearer of the responsibility in providing benefits in case the unemployment insurance funds dried up.

The primary purpose of the unemployment insurance programme established by Document 77 of 1986 was to facilitate reform of the SOEs. However, due to the fact that SOEs were not given a free hand, during the whole latter part of the 1980s, to dismiss their 'laid-off employees' on a large scale, actual unemployment beneficiaries were few in number. A large part of the unemployment funds were accumulated as a result. When reform of the SOEs began to speed up in the early 1990s, the number of involuntarily displaced workers due to enterprise reforms increased rapidly. It was clear that further expansion of the unemployment insurance programme was required to support a greater number of the unemployed. The State Council issued thus, in 1993, 'Regulations on Unemployment

Insurance for Employees in SOEs' (Document 110).

Document 110 of 1993 made several changes to the previous unemployment insurance programme. First, the coverage was extended from the previously four types of workers to seven types of workers. The resulting scheme covered almost all kinds of workers in SOEs who have lost their jobs due to various reasons, except for temporary workers and workers who resigned on a voluntary basis or terminated their contract ahead of time.

Second, benefit levels were changed from the previous 60-75 per cent of the standard wage to 120-150 per cent of the social relief administered by local civil affairs departments, while the duration of receiving the benefits remained the same.

Third, the base for enterprises to contribute was changed from the total amount of standard wages to that of total wages, and contribution rates were readjusted to 0.6-1 per cent of total wages. Local governments were allowed to determine the exact rate of enterprise contributions.

Fourth, the pooling base was changed from provincial pooling to city or county-based pooling, due to difficulties encountered in the implementation of provincially unified unemployment insurance intended in Document 77 of 1986.

Fifth, Document 110 of 1993 put more emphasis on re-employment services in that local governments were allowed to determine and extract a certain percentage of the funds for providing training programmes and financial assistance for the unemployed.

Finally, the document also provided that penalties would be applied to individuals and agencies that commit embezzlement or use the funds in illegal ways.

The implementation of Document 110 of 1993 was an improvement over the unemployment insurance programme established by Document 77 of 1986 in that more unemployed persons managed to receive the appropriate benefits. In 1994, the number of beneficiaries rose abruptly to 1.94 million, exceeding the total number of beneficiaries for the previous seven years. However, as the coverage of the programme continued to be limited within the state sector, the number of those covered actually declined since the mid-1990s when a higher percentage of the urban labour force shifted to work from the state to the non-state sector. From 1995 to 1998, the number of covered employees decreased from 82.38 million to 79.28 million. There was a fear that the unemployment insurance programme would ultimately become insolvent if it continued to be limited within the state sector. There was therefore a need to expand the funding base.

By the mid-1990s, unemployment was known to exist not only in the state or public sector; employees in the private sector and enterprises with other types of ownership have also been facing the danger of losing their jobs. From a social equity point of view, it was then argued that unemployment insurance should be made available for employees in enterprises of all types of ownership. Besides, failure to provide unemployment benefits for all the workers who have involuntarily lost their jobs might pose a threat to social stability. Based on the above, the State Council issued in January 1999, 'Regulations on Unemployment Insurance', which paved the road for the further development of unemployment insurance in China.

The regulations made the following changes to the unemployment insurance programme. First, the goal of unemployment insurance was defined as a support for an acceptable living standard and the promotion of re-employment for the unemployed.

Second, the coverage of unemployment insurance was extended to include all types of employees and formal work organizations in cities, except for governmental organs and their workers. Local governments were allowed to extend the coverage to other types of urban labour force such as employees in mass organizations, non-governmental organizations, self-employed households and their employees. The expanded coverage substantially increased the funding base and led to a net increase of 5.7 million employees eligible for benefits.

Third, contribution rates were raised for enterprises from 0.6-1 per cent to 2 per cent of the total wages, and employees were also required to make an individual contribution of 1 per cent of the total wage. Thus, the total contributions for unemployment insurance amounted to 3 per cent of the wages. The increase in enterprise contribution rates and the requirement for individuals to contribute were two of the most important changes in the new unemployment insurance system. This was done mainly in consideration of two factors: One was that the number of unemployed employees was expected to continue to increase. The other factor was that unemployment insurance funds would in future be used for providing one-third of the funds for the laid-off formal employees.

Fourth, the duration of benefits was differentiated into three grades, instead of the previously two grades, based on the number of years the worker had contributed to the funds, that is, the length of covered services prior to unemployment. A one-year fully covered service was the qualifying criteria for the unemployed to be eligible for benefits. The maximum period for an unemployed worker to live on unemployment benefits was 24 months, if he or she had over 10 years of covered services (instead of 5 years of service), 18 months for 5 to less than 10 years, and 12 months for 1 to less than 5 years. An unemployed worker could get 60-75 per cent of the standard wage during the first 12 months of unemployment and 50 per cent for the remaining 12 months. The exact level of benefits was to be determined by local governments according to individual situations, provided that it was below the standard for minimum wage and above that for poverty relief, which varied considerably across regions and localities. The unemployed living on unemployment benefits could also apply for poverty relief if qualified.

Fifth, items of benefits and expenses covered by unemployment funds were also changed. During the benefit period, an unemployed would be provided for five items of benefits: (1) unemployment benefits; (2) medical care expenses; (3) funeral expenses and survivors' compensation; (4) subsidies for accessing services of training and job introduction; and (5) and other related expenses on a case by case basis. Compared with the items of expenses contained in Document 110 of 1993, two important changes were made. One was that the funds would not be made available for providing financial assistance for the unemployed to re-start or organize economic activities. This item of support was eliminated because it tended to be abused by local authorities and proved to be ineffective. Another change was that administrative expenses were to be appropriated by the government through separate channels, instead of allowing funds management agencies to deduct a certain percentage from the unemployment funds as administrative expenses.

Finally, the regulations also made changes to the base of pooling. In cities directly under the central government and those with independent municipal jurisdiction, unified pooling at the city level was required. In other localities, local governments were allowed to determine the scope and base of pooling.

The implementation of the new regulations has considerably increased the number of covered employees. The number of covered employees increased from 79.28 million in 1998 to 91.78 million a year later. It was estimated that in 1998 the number of employees eligible for coverage under the new regulations was about 137 million, but of this number only 58 per cent were actually covered by unemployment insurance. There is, therefore, still a long way to go before unemployment insurance can be fully implemented.

As mentioned before, the provision for laid-off formal employees constitutes a special part of the social security system in China. Up to mid-1990s, laid-off formal employees were generally provided for by the enterprises where they had worked, while local governments supplemented by designing various preferential policies such as obtaining for them bank loans, organizing training programmes and job seeking services, and encouraging other enterprises to hire them. As the number of laid-off formal employees increased rapidly in the latter part of the 1990s, in order to maintain social stability, local governments were required to set up re-employment service centers at different administrative levels and in enterprises where large numbers of employees were displaced. These centers were responsible to provide financial assistance, training and job seeking services for the laid-off formal employees.

Thus, by the late 1990s, a three-channel financing system, comprising the enterprises, the government and the society as a whole, has been developed throughout the country to provide support for the displaced workers. In actual practice, contributions from the enterprises made up a large proportion of the funds required and the sum was based on the number of laid-off employees coming from them. The role of the government consisted of adopting the various preferential policies and subsidizing the operation of the re-employment centers. Recently, measures have also been taken to have one third of the funds for laid-off formal employees coming from unemployment insurance funds, so that the laid-off formal employees could have small capitals to start their own economic activities.

Despite the multiple financing method, the majority of the laid-off formal employees still failed to receive the necessary services and financial support, particularly when their employing enterprises were running at a loss or were unable to make their contributions. Also, though the re-employment service centers were the officially designated places from where laid-off formal employees could receive financial support and other services, most could not honour their obligations. It was reported that in 1997 China had a total number of 6.34 million laid-off formal employees, and among them, 5.64 million (89%) were not registered in the re-employment service centres and 3.1 million (49%) did not receive any financial assistance (*China Labour Statistical Yearbook 1998*, p. 432).

By the end of March 1998, laid-off formal employees who were receiving support in re-employment service centers represented only 12.6 per cent. Following a meeting held by the central government in May 1998, which was called to deal with the problem of laid-off formal employees, the Labour and Social Security Ministry took some urgent measures to improve the situation. As a result, the number of covered employees in the re-employment service centres increased to 21.9 per cent by the end of 1998 (*China Labour and Social Security Ministry, 1999b*).

In addition, to further improve the provision and support for laid-off formal employees, the Central Committee of the CCP and the State Council jointly issued in June 1998 'An Announcement on Implementing Basic Security and Re-employment Services for Laid-off Formal Employees in SOEs' (Document 10). The document set out three major objectives regarding the provision for laid-off formal employees, which were to be realized by the end of 1998.

The first was that all enterprises which had laid-off formal employees were required to set up a re-employment service centre or a similar structure, so that all laid-off employees would be assisted. The centres were responsible for delivering living allowances to and making social insurance contributions on behalf of the laid-off formal employees, and helping them to obtain training and to find jobs.

Second, all laid-off employees should receive the full amount of the living allowance as was stipulated by the government. To ensure that funds for laid-off formal employees were readily available, the document reaffirmed the previous three-channel financing method in more specific terms. That is, enterprises, the government and the unemployment insurance funds were each to bear one-third of the living allowances for laid-off formal employees.

Third, each re-employment service centre should aim at helping half of the laid-off formal employees to find jobs within a year.

Hence, by the end of the 1990s, the problem of unemployment has largely been tackled, with measures installed to assist the unemployed. It is obvious that in tackling the problem of unemployment, China has not only taken into consideration the need of the unemployed, but also the necessity of continuing the social obligations of the SOEs, and the importance of maintaining social stability. In a way, the various measures, including the provisions for the laid-off employees and the hard-core unemployed, should in theory be more than sufficient in giving the displaced workers the necessary support. However, what has been written on paper does not always represent what has actually happened in China and it would be sometime before the regulations on unemployment insurance could be implemented in full.

PART THREE

THE GUANGZHOU EXPERIENCE FOR THE NATION

8 The First City to Experience Economic Reform

The Administrative Structure of Guangzhou Government

Being the capital city of the Guangdong Province, Guangzhou is the biggest coastal city in South China, covering a total area of 7,434.4 square kilometers. Situated in the southern tip of the Province and north of the Pearl River Delta, adjacent to Hong Kong and Macao, like the three points of a triangle, Guangzhou has traditionally been referred to as the 'Southern Gate' to China. Guangzhou is also known as the hometown for the overseas Chinese, and before 1997, for the Hong Kong and Macao residents as well. Hence, ever since the inception of the economic reforms in 1978, Guangzhou has always been the first, among the cities in China, to experiment with the reforms, and is also the first to have changed its social security provisions for the enterprise employees.

The administrative structure of Guangzhou follows the national uniform pattern, with a two-level government system and a three-level administrative structure. Hence, governmental structure is established at both the city and the district levels. The municipal government oversees the district governments, with each district consisting of a number of streets, and each street covering several residents' committees. Although not forming part of the government, the street offices administer the residents' committees on behalf of the district government. As at 1997, Guangzhou was made up of 8 districts and 4 county-level cities; the 8 district governments administered a total of 98 streets and 22 townships, which were held responsible for 1,435 residents' committees and 274 village committees. The 4 county-level cities had under their jurisdiction 7 streets, 54 townships, 144 residents' committees, and 1,000 village committees.

At the end of 1997, Guangzhou had a population of over 6.66 million people. Between 1952 and 1990, the population in Guangzhou had more than doubled, increasing from 2.72 million to 5.94 million. Since 1991, the number of people has been growing at a more moderate speed, with a net increase of about 100,000 persons per year. The slowing down of the population increase is largely due to the continued decrease in the birth rate since the early 1990s (Table 8.1).

Table 8.1: Population growth in Guangzhou since 1957

Year	Population	Birth rate (%)	Death rate (%)	Natural increase (%)
1957	3377586	39.49	7.12	32.37
1962	3702454	38.78	6.80	31.98
1965	3985070	27.01	5.25	21.76
1970	4185363	23.79	5.46	18.33
1975	4591000	16.94	5.95	10.99
1980	5018638	16.25	5.57	10.68
1985	5449820	16.59	5.36	11.23
1990	5942534	14.97	5.49	9.48
1991	6022186	13.15	5.09	8.06
1992	6122016	13.11	5.53	7.58
1993	6236647	13.35	5.60	7.75
1994	6370241	12.47	5.29	7.18
1995	6467115	11.82	5.57	6.25
1996	6560508	12.03	5.71	6.32
1997	6664862	11.37	5.40	5.97

Source: 'The Statistical Yearbook of Guangzhou 1998'.

Since the mid-1980s, a significant feature in the population change of Guangzhou has been the increase in the size of the non-local population, which was made up mostly by non-local workers. Spurred by the open-door policy and the rapid economic development in Guangzhou, it is known that increasing number of labourers have been 'floating' from various parts of the country into Guangzhou to seek employment. >From 1986 to 1997, the number of migrant workers increased from 474,000 to 1.7 million. Migrant workers in Guangzhou are engaged in various kinds of economic activities, including industry, agriculture, commerce, and services (Table 8.2), and they have no doubt played an important role in its economic development.

Table 8.2: Non-local residents in Guangzhou in the 1990s

Year	Non-local residents (persons)	Places of origin (%) Within province	Outside province
1992	1455472	46.31	45.47
1994	1271576	37.54	61.20
1995	1336387	37.00	60.41
1996	1708541	38.13	60.88
1997	1700000	41.00	58.21

Sources: 'The Statistical Yearbook of Guangzhou', various years.

Economic and Social Changes

On the economic side, since the Third Plenary Session of the Eleventh Central Committee Meeting of the CCP held in 1978, which decided on the beginning of the economic reforms, Guangzhou has been experiencing rapid and steady economic growth. From 1980 to 1997, GDP in Guangzhou grew from 5.75 billion to 164.63 billion, while per capita GDP grew from 907 *yuan* in 1978 to 24,895 yuan in 1997 (*The Statistical Yearbook of Guangzhou 1998,* p. 21). The annual growth rate of GDP averaged 14.33 per cent between 1979 and 1997, and 18.06 per cent between 1991 and 1997. While the first and secondary sectors dominated the economy during the planned economy era before 1978, the tertiary sector has recorded the most rapid growth since the beginning of the economic reforms. Between 1980 and 1997, the output value of the tertiary sector increased from 34.64 per cent to 48.25 per cent of the total, while that of the first and secondary sectors steadily declined (Table 8.3).

Another noteworthy change in the economy of Guangzhou was that the non-state economic sector has become the new direction of economic development in place of the public ownership economy. In terms of GDP by types of ownership, the percentage of GDP represented by the state sector has been declining throughout the reform period. In 1996, the state sector accounted for only 20.5 per cent of the GDP, various joint ventures for 43.5 per cent, and enterprises with other types of ownership for 36 per cent. In 1998, it was envisaged that the percentage of GDP accounted for by the state sector would further reduce to 10 per cent, with joint ventures increasing to 50-55 per cent and enterprises with other types of ownership to 40 per cent by 2000 (*Government of Guangzhou 1998*, Vol. 5, p. 43).

Table 8.3: GDP growth by different sectors in Guangzhou, 1980-97 (RMB 10,000)

Year	GDP	Output value (%)		
		Primary Sector	Secondary Sector	Tertiary Sector
1980	575497	10.85	54.52	34.63
1985	1243623	9.69	52.92	37.39
1990	3195952	8.05	42.65	49.30
1991	3866741	7.29	46.53	46.18
1992	5107027	6.98	47.25	45.77
1993	7408369	6.42	47.48	46.10
1994	9761829	6.21	46.79	47.00
1995	12430697	5.91	46.67	47.42
1996	14449358	5.62	46.74	47.64
1997	16462567	5.21	46.54	48.25

Source: 'The Statistical Yearbook of Guangzhou 1998', p. 28.

The pattern of change in the gross industrial output value also shows that the non-state sector has been increasing its important in the economic development of Guangzhou. Gross industrial output value rose from 10.60 billion in 1982 to 237.54 billion in 1997, making an average increase of 16.26 per cent between 1979 and 1997 and 22.98 per cent between 1991 and 1997. Per capita gross industrial output value also increased from 1,586 yuan in 1978 to 35,922 yuan in 1997. In terms of ownership, between 1982 and 1997, the percentage of gross industrial output value decreased from 74.07 to 25.37 in the state sector and from 24.11 to 8.77 in the collectively owned sector, while that of enterprises with other types of ownership increased from 1.83 to 65.86 (Table 8.4).

Table 8.4: Gross industrial output value by types of ownership in Guangzhou, 1982-97 (10,000 yuan)

Year	GOV of industry	State Sector (%)	Collective Sector (%)	Other Sector (%)
1982	1060459	74.07	24.11	1.83
1983	1187130	74.23	23.82	1.95
1984	1333609	73.55	24.40	2.05
1985	1703824	67.74	27.75	4.51
1986	1779745	65.59	25.45	8.97
1987	2149315	62.51	26.05	11.44
1988	2637817	58.57	26.62	14.81
1989	4071472	59.68	17.61	22.71
1990	4424437	57.80	15.78	26.43
1991	5794842	54.88	14.73	30.39
1992	7905237	50.55	14.48	34.98
1993	11422184	40.74	14.20	45.06
1994	14921455	31.39	13.00	55.61
1995	17224948	25.25	10.23	64.52
1996	20685796	20.53	9.38	70.09
1997	23753915	25.37	8.77	65.86

Sources: 'The Statistical Yearbook of Guangzhou', various years.

Because of its edge over other cities, in terms of its geographical location and the quality of its human resources, Guangzhou came out in 1992 as the third among the 'top 50 cities in China in terms of comprehensive economic strength', ranking only after Shanghai and Beijing. It was further appraised as one of the 'top 40 cities with the best environment for investment' (Li, 1994). At the end of 1997, Guangzhou ranked third after Shanghai (336.02 billion yuan) and Beijing (181.01 billion) in terms of GDP and third after Shanghai (560.63 billion yuan) and Tianjin (283.82 billion yuan) in terms of gross industrial output value (*The Statistical Yearbook of Guangzhou 1998*, p. 525).

One direct benefit of the rapid growth of the economy on the residents of Guangzhou was the continued increase in their incomes, which rose per capita from 442 yuan in 1978 to 10,495 yuan in 1997, being the highest in China (Table 8.5). In 1997, per capita consumption in Guangzhou reached 8,767 yuan, higher than that by Shanghai and Beijing residents (*The Guangzhou Yearbook 1998*, p. 375). Housing conditions for urban residents in Guangzhou have also showed marked improvements. From 1978 to 1997, per capita housing areas increased from 3.93 to 11.67 square meters, with 56 per cent of the residents owning their own houses (*The Guangzhou Yearbook 1998*, p. 375).

Table 8.5: Average income and housing areas of Guangzhou residents, 1978-97

Year	Average income (yuan) Housing areas (m^2)	(%)
1978	442	3.93
1980	555	3.97
1985	1047	6.62
1990	2593	7.99
1995	8553	9.61
1996	9379	10.08
1997	10,495.4	11.67

Sources: 'The Guangzhou Yearbook', various years.

Finally, savings by urban residents in Guangzhou have been growing. The total amount of savings by urban residents increased from 1.36 billion yuan in 1982 to 134.63 billion yuan in 1997 (Table 8.6), with per capita savings from 117 yuan in 1978 to 19,712 yuan in 1996 (*The Statistical Yearbook of Guangzhou 1997*, p. 17).

Table 8.6: Savings by urban residents in Guangzhou since 1982 (10,000 yuan)

Year	Total savings
1982	135,748
1984	225,468
1986	424,351
1988	708,627
1990	1,420,432
1992	2,612,308
1994	5,099,020
1995	7,854,269
1996	10,845,770
1997	13,462,824

Sources: 'The Statistical Yearbook of Guangzhou', various years.

In summary, Guangzhou has taken full advantage of the economic reforms that started in 1978, and combined with its geographical advantage, being most adjacent to Hong Kong, its own economic development is most spectacular. The rapid increase in economic activities has also brought about substantial improvements in the livelihood of Guangzhou residents. However, economic growth in Guangzhou has implied, as in other cities in China, a dismantling of the former planned economic structure. In transforming the traditionally socialist planned economy into a socialist market economy, reforms have also turned the traditionally public ownership economy into a mixed economy with multiple types of ownership. In other words, economic reforms in Guangzhou have been accompanied by a decline in the importance of the SOEs. And in the course of reforming the SOEs, policies that would facilitate the transfer of the SOEs from governmental agencies to independent market-oriented economic entities have to be brought in, which would often imply a revision of the social security provisions. The following chapters would examine the challenges that have faced the Guangzhou workers as they moved from total dependence on the government to having their incomes coming from the market.

9 Dismantling the State-owned Enterprises in Guangzhou

The Three Phases of SOE Reforms

In parallel with the national economic reform agenda, SOEs reforms in Guangzhou have also undergone three major phases. The first phase lasted from 1979 to 1984, during which the theme was to expand the autonomy of the SOEs and to return the profits to enterprises. In the second phase, spanning from 1985 to 1993, the focus was to experiment with the attempt to separate SOEs from the government. Since 1994, though the goal of economic reform shifted to the building of modern enterprises, efforts have still been concentrating on redefining the relationship between SOEs and the government.

1979-84: Decentralization of Authority and Returning Profits to Enterprises

Economic reforms in Guangzhou started in response to the call of the central government for readjusting the economic sector, which was approved in the Third Plenary Session of the Eleventh Central Committee Meeting of the CCP held in 1978. The initial economic reforms proposed by the central government included attempts to rectify mistakes made during the planned economy era, such as placing an undue emphasis on heavy industry. It was decided that the living standard of the people must come first in an attempt to develop the economy.

Following the decision of the CCP in 1978, the Guangzhou government passed three measures to implement the reform policies.

First, readjustments were made to the industrial structure by giving priority to the development of light and textile industries.

Second, old enterprises were technologically transformed, with losing and inefficient ones being either closed down, merged, or made to change their lines of production. As a result, an annual increase of 9.3 per cent was made, between 1978 and 1982, in the total industrial output.

Third, capital investment priorities were shifted, the first time since the founding of the PRC, from infrastructure and heavy industry projects to light industry, agriculture, public utilities, housing and educational ones, all of which have a direct impact on the livelihood of the people. After the readjustment, the percentage of municipal non-production investment increased from 29.2 per cent in 1978 to 55.3 per cent in 1982, while that of production investment decreased from 70.8 per cent to 44.7 per cent. This change was understood as an effort of the Guangzhou government to raise the living standard of the people (*Guangzhou Yearbook 1983*).

Meanwhile, SOEs reforms in Guangzhou followed the 'special and flexible implementation policies' allowed for Guangzhou by the central government. Starting from 1979, the Guangzhou government adopted three measures to reform its SOEs in accordance with the policies designed by the State Council.

The first measure was to expand the autonomy of the SOEs, in line with the central directive of 'decentralization of authority and returning profits to enterprises'. Experiments were first conducted in selected SOEs such as the Sewing Machine Company, the No.1 Textile Factory of Guangzhou and the Chemical Plant. These enterprises were given the autonomy in production, distribution, and management. In specific terms, they were allowed to retain and use a certain percentage of their profits, design their own management structure, set their own production targets, and administer their own employment policy.

The second and related measure was the experimentation of 'taxation replacing profits', by which enterprises would be taxed instead of handing over their profits to the government. The reform was carried out in two steps. The first step was conducted between 1980 and 1983, during which 10 selected enterprises were allowed to retain a certain percentage of their profits after taxation. However, these enterprises must be responsible for their losses and the state would no longer provide them with subsidies. Starting from 1983, the experiment was gradually extended to other profit-making enterprises. In 1984, the previous practice of enterprises handing over both profits and taxes to government was thoroughly replaced by taxation alone, which was the second step of 'taxation replacing profits'.

The third measure was the introduction of various forms of fiscal responsibility systems. It took place from 1979 to 1981. After 1981, the individual responsibility system was gradually changed to include the entire sector, with enterprises in each industrial sector becoming a single unit to be responsible for their profits and losses. By 1984, most SOEs in Guangzhou had adopted the sector responsibility system. Under the new arrangement, SOEs began to have a larger degree of autonomy in planning their economic activities and in distributing benefits to employees. The performance of SOEs became thus the most important factor in determining the amount of funds available for further production and development and also the levels of wages, welfare and bonuses for employees. In this way, there was greater incentive for SOEs to remain competitive. Under the sector responsibility system, the Guangzhou government was also less concerned about the performance of each individual enterprise, as enterprises belonging to the same sector would be watching the performance of each other.

The most important effect of the SOEs reforms carried out during the first phase was that the performance of the enterprises was directly related to the material gains of the employees. In contrast to the former practice of 'unified collection and expenditure', in which enterprises obtained their funds from the state in accordance with the amount of their wage bill, the implementation of the economic responsibility system had, at least, partly removed the syndrome of 'eating out of the big rice pot'. Another noteworthy result of the SOEs reforms was that enterprises improved in their productivity and, for the first time since the founding of the PRC, were in a position to increase the wages of their employees.

1985-93: Separating Government from Enterprises

The mid-1980s was a period when rigorous reforms took place throughout China. In contrast to the previous reforms that were initiated by the preferential policies of the central government for special enterprises, reforms in the latter part of the 1980s were implemented with the intention of separating enterprises from the government.

The dominant theme of SOEs reforms during the second phase was concentrated on 'delinking ownership from management'. In 1984, Guangzhou became one of the 14 coastal cities to adopt an open-door policy. This would allow the cities a more flexible approach in their economic policies; the central government would also decentralize the authority to the municipal governments so as to achieve 'separating government from enterprises'. Beginning from 1985, in response to the State Council's 'Regulations on Further Expanding Enterprise Autonomy' issued in 1984, SOEs reforms in Guangzhou went into full strength.

In brief, the focus of the reforms during this period aimed at an overhaul transformation of the operation of the SOEs, so that they could become more efficient, although they were still owned by the state. In actual practice, the reforms consisted of the following three.

First was the expansion of the autonomy of the SOEs, with the objective of enabling the SOEs to truly become economic entities, independent of the government. SOEs were thus given greater freedom in recruiting workers, in distributing wages, bonuses and other rewards, in managing production, in designing management structures, in dealing with fixed assets, in improving technology, and in handling imports and exports.

Together with the reforms in the labour and wage system in the mid-1980s, which established multiple types of labour and wage structures, enterprises were given autonomy in designing their own remunerative systems, and to recruit employees under contract, temporary, or other arrangements according to individual situations.

In 1988, in order to put into effect the Enterprise Law, the Guangzhou government issued 'Regulations on Deepening Reforms and Invigorating Enterprises', which were designed to expand the autonomy of the enterprises. Enterprise autonomy was further realized in such areas as production, distribution, fund usage, personnel and labour administration, and the handling of imports and exports. To improve the efficiency of the enterprises, the Guangzhou government also reduced the number of administrative hurdles that enterprises had to overcome, by either removing or merging the bureaus in control of the enterprises.

Second, ways of separating government from enterprises were explored. During this phase, various responsibility systems continued to be adopted, including contracting, leasing, and particularly the system of overall responsibility by managers. By the end of 1988, over 90 per cent of SOEs in Guangzhou operated under different forms of responsibility systems. To improve the system of contracting and leasing, open tender and mortgage were introduced, in accordance with the Enterprise Law. By the end of 1989, 99 per cent of state-owned industrial enterprises, 97 per cent of large and medium size state-owned commercial enterprises and all of the small state-owned commercial enterprises were either contracted out or leased. Most of the contracting and leasing took place through either open tender or mortgage by managers and/or employees. In 1991, when the second round of contracting and leasing was completed, it differed from the previous one in that financial viability was no longer the only consideration, managerial performance and developmental potentials were also counted as important indicators in evaluating the performance of the enterprises.

Finally, competition was introduced and encouraged within individual enterprises. Major measures adopted included 'competitive bidding', 'internal contracting', 'merit employment' and 'optimizing regrouping'. Competitive bidding was practiced for managerial positions at different levels, by which applicants either inside or outside the enterprises could compete for the positions. Internal contracting implies that responsibilities for economic performance were divided among and born by individual work units within an enterprise, and each work unit would be required to maintain its own accounting. Merit employment was a method of internal competition among employees, by which continued employment in an enterprise depended on the performance of individual workers. Optimizing regrouping was the method used by enterprises to restructure and select employees according to the need of the enterprise concerned, in contrast to the former practice that work was arranged according to the need of employees. Selected workers would then remain in employment, while those who were regrouped out would become surplus workers.

As the number of surplus workers rapidly increased since the beginning of the 1990s, re-arrangement for work became one of the most difficult tasks in SOEs reforms. As implicit unemployment and underemployment had been a conspicuous feature in most SOEs during the planned economy era, as a result of the policy of 'full employment and low wages', the emergence of increasing number of surplus workers became inevitable as contracting, leasing or other responsibility systems took effect. In 1989, to prevent conflicts arising between contractors and workers over matters such as employment and distribution of benefits, the Guangzhou government issued regulations to control the incomes for contractors and managers. At the same time, enterprises were encouraged to establish 'community of mutual benefits', by which contractors or managers and the enterprise trade unions would sign mutual protection contracts.

Market-oriented reforms also took place simultaneously with SOEs reforms in the latter part of the 1980s. By the end of 1988, markets of the various means of production, such as steel, timber, chemicals, and transportation vehicles were established, resulting in about 75 per cent of production means being allocated through the markets. In the following years, markets were set up for labour, funds, technology and real estates. The price system also underwent substantial changes, with governmental control over the prices of the means of production and living gradually relaxed. By the end of 1992, over 98 per cent of the total retail sales for mass commodities, 95 per cent of the total sales for the means of production, and 70 per cent in the third sector were regulated through the market.

1994- : Establishing Modern Enterprises

Along with the implementation of various forms of responsibility and contracting systems, aimed at separating enterprises from the government, SOEs reforms gradually shifted their focus to turning existing enterprises into modern ones. The direction of change followed the decision made by the central government in 1993, in which modern enterprises were defined as shareholding companies or organizations. Since 1994, in accordance with the reform principles outlined by the central government, SOEs reforms in Guangzhou were represented by attempts to convert enterprises, especially the losing and inefficient ones, into various forms of shareholding companies.

In fact, SOEs reforms in mid-1980s had already included attempts to deal with economically inefficient enterprises through such methods as mergers, change of the production line, or forcing them to declare themselves bankrupt. Between 1986 and 1991, 3,134 losing enterprises were merged with 106 profit-making ones. In 1993, 'difficulty alleviation and organizational transformation' experiments were tried out to raise the productivity of losing enterprises and 152 enterprises were thus selected by the Guangzhou government. These enterprises had either been closed down or merged with profit-making ones. Some had been required to change their production lines or to declare themselves bankrupt. In 1995, the number of enterprises included in the experiment increased to 205. Furthermore, some enterprises were encouraged to set up joint ventures with foreign investors and 27 enterprises were thus turned into joint ventures, absorbing over 100 million yuan of foreign investment.

On top of the above, the Guangzhou government further encouraged some losing enterprises to engage in real estate development. As a profitable business heavily subsidized by the government, real estate development provided a chance for enterprises to generate funds for the purposes of paying their debts or purchasing new technology. Finally, stockholding companies were created as another way to deal with the economically constrained enterprises. Stockholding had been tried as early as the mid-1980s. Between 1985 and 1987, stockholding was experimented in 17 enterprises where employees were encouraged to become shareholders of their own enterprises. The purpose of the initial experiments was to deal with the problem of fund shortage and to encourage employees to invest in their own enterprises. In 1992, a special group was set up by the Guangzhou government to design policies for the formation of stockholding and limited liability companies. By 1993, the number of limited liability companies reached 41. In addition, 120 stockholding enterprises were established, 5 to be listed in Shenzhen and Shanghai stock markets.

Meanwhile, profit-making enterprises in Guangzhou also underwent a series of reforms. One of the measures employed was to form corporate groups in the form of stockholding companies. Starting 1987, in order to increase competitiveness, enterprises with development potentials formed themselves into corporate entities with unified production, marketing and trading plans. From 1987 to 1995, the number of registered corporate companies increased from 19 to 75, but few of them were large ones. In 1995, 46 enterprises in Guangzhou were selected to become modern enterprises, in accordance with the criteria defined by the central government. Furthermore, the Guangzhou government put up a proposal in 1995 that to increase local competitiveness, 5 corporate groups with 10 billion yuan of annual sales output, 8 with 5 billion yuan and 10 with 3 billion yuan would appear in Guangzhou within 10 years.

Reform of the Labour System

Same as other cities in China, the permanent labour system adopted in Guangzhou during the planned economy era was widely regarded as one of the major causes leading to low morale of the workers and the inefficiency of the enterprises. With the aim of creating a labour system conducive to economic productivity, Guangzhou began to reform its permanent labour system as early as 1977, a year before the beginning of the economic reforms. Earliest reforms of the labour system in Guangzhou started with the government expanding employment channels and allowing workers to find work on their own. Those without work could then look for jobs through multiple channels, including the employment service provided by the local labour department, voluntarily engaging themselves in small businesses, and becoming self-employed individuals. From 1980 to 1986, the Guangzhou government established 777 collectively owned labour service companies at different administrative levels, providing employment assistance for over 43,000 people.

Since the early 1980s, three major changes have occurred in the labour system of Guangzhou.

First, employment became increasingly diversified and complex, with contract labour increasingly replacing permanent workers. As elsewhere in China, the urban labour force in Guangzhou is divided into employees and formal employees. Among the formal employees, that covered 83 per cent of urban employees in Guangzhou in 1997, employment status was further divided into contract, temporary and permanent employees. Contract labour was first experimented in Guangzhou in 1983. In the beginning, it was practiced in a number of SOEs and district collectively owned enterprises on an experimental basis. In 1986, when the State Council issued Document 77 which formally established the system of contract labour in SOEs, enterprises in Guangzhou were allowed to recruit contract, temporary or seasonal, and migrant workers according to individual conditions. New workers were thus employed on a contractual basis, with clearly defined rights and obligations. Since then, the trend was that, on the one hand, contract workers were gradually replacing permanent employees in SOEs and collectively owned enterprises, and, on the other, permanent employees were gradually brought under the contractual arrangement.

At the end of 1987, the number of contract workers in Guangzhou reached more than 100,000, and increased to over 210,000 in 1992. Starting from the early 1990s, the Guangzhou government began to put into implementation 'contract employment for all employees' in a number of enterprises, such as Nanfang Building Limited-liability Company, Nanfang Flour Limited-liability Company, and Guangzhou Cold Storage Plant. In 1994, the Guangzhou government issued regulations requiring all enterprises in Guangzhou to adopt the system of 'contract labour for all employees', including the SOEs, collectively owned enterprises, and government institutions. At the end of 1995, 677,000 permanent workers in 11,200 enterprises were converted into contract workers, representing 96 per cent of the permanent workers in Guangzhou. From 1994 to 1997, the percentage of permanent workers in Guangzhou declined from 70 per cent to 36 per cent, while contract workers increased from 12.68 per cent to 48.46 per cent, and temporary workers decreased from 17.33 per cent to 15.48 per cent. Table 9.1 presents the distribution of formal employees, permanent workers, contract workers and temporary workers in Guangzhou between 1994 and 1997.

Table 9.1: Distribution of formal, permanent, contract and temporary workers in Guangzhou, 1994-97

Year	Formal employees	Permanent workers No.	(%)	Contract workers No.	(%)	Temporary workers No.	(%)
1994	2093585	1465555	70.00	265296	12.68	362734	17.33
1995	2082361	907109	43.56	793709	38.12	381543	18.32
1996	2028859	731948	36.08	959661	47.30	337250	16.62
1997	1998075	720428	36.06	968299	48.46	309348	15.48

Sources: 'The Statistical Yearbook of Guangzhou', various years.

Second, since economic reforms started, employment opportunities shifted from the primary and secondary sectors to the tertiary sector. From 1980 to 1997, the percentage of the labour force in the primary sector declined from 40.23 per cent to 21.77 per cent, with that in the secondary sector fluctuating between 33.55 per cent to 38.04 per cent, and that in the tertiary sector increased from 26.22 per cent to 40.19 per cent. Table 9.2 gives the distribution of the labour force in Guangzhou by the three sectors from 1980 to 1997.

Table 9.2: Distribution of employees by the three sectors in Guangzhou, 1980-97

Year	Total no. of employees	No. of employees (%) Primary sector	Secondary sector	Tertiary sector
1980	2750467	40.23	33.55	26.22
1985	3134739	31.26	37.66	31.08
1990	3411513	28.24	36.40	35.36
1991	3559487	27.59	36.80	35.61
1992	3736162	26.24	37.82	35.94
1993	3847821	24.81	37.89	37.21
1994	3831732	23.76	37.14	39.10
1995	3913824	23.38	36.41	40.21
1996	3928907	23.46	34.72	41.82
1997	4282130	21.77	38.04	40.19

Source: 'The Statistical Yearbook of Guangzhou 1998', p. 54.

Third, the urban labour force shifted from the public to the non-public sector. This trend was clearly reflected in that both the number and the proportion of urban employees in public-owned enterprises had declined while that in the non-public sector, including owners and employees in private enterprises and individual commercial and industrial households had rapidly increased. In 1997, the total number of urban employees in Guangzhou reached about 2.4 million, of which over 1.27 million (53.14%) worked in state-owned units, 0.37 million (15.35%) in collectively owned units, and 0.73 million (30.68%) in enterprises with other types of ownership. Although the state sector remained to be the largest employer, employment opportunities have definitely been shifting towards the non-public sector. Table 9.3 presents the distribution of employees in the urban areas of Guangzhou, from 1982 to 1997, by types of ownership.

Table 9.3: Distribution of employees by types of ownership in Guangzhou, 1982-97

Year	Total no. of employees	State-owned	Collectively owned	Collectively owned
1982	1835209	73.40	24.30	2.31
1983	1853222	73.11	23.46	3.43
1984	1888940	70.12	25.22	4.66
1985	1931429	70.72	23.94	5.35
1986	1991996	70.98	23.10	5.92
1987	2043346	71.01	22.25	6.74
1988	1965365	70.92	21.31	7.78
1989	1953167	69.96	20.29	9.75
1990	2002552	68.18	19.97	11.85
1991	2114056	65.84	20.77	13.39
1992	2205681	63.51	20.84	15.65
1993	2302914	60.14	20.56	19.30
1994	2360367	58.46	20.52	21.02
1995	2378885	56.52	18.89	24.59
1996	2377076	52.27	17.73	27.00
1997	2395375	53.14	15.35	30.68

Sources: 'The Statistical Yearbook of Guangzhou', various years.

The shifting of the labour force from the public to the non-public sector had also been manifested in the decreasing number of formal employees; those employed in state-owned and collectively owned enterprises. With rapid economic development, the number of employees in Guangzhou increased from 2.75 million in 1980 to 4.28 million in 1997. However, as from 1993, especially as a result of the reform of the SOEs, whereby enterprises improved their efficiency through reducing the number of employees, both the number and the percentage of formal employees had decreased. From 1993 to 1997, the number and percentage of formal employees decreased from 2.1 million, or 54.71 per cent of the urban labour force, to less than 2 million, or 46.66 per cent. Table 9.4 gives the changes in the distribution of employees in Guangzhou, especially in relation to the percentage of formal employees, between 1980 and 1997.

Table 9.4: Distribution of employees in Guangzhou, 1980-97

Year	Employees	Urban employees in the non-public sector (%)	Formal Employees (%)	Rural Workers (%)
1980	2750467	56.92	42.20	0.88
1985	3134739	56.03	41.81	2.16
1986	3219162	56.19	41.60	2.21
1987	3289666	56.13	41.58	2.29
1988	3339840	56.29	41.15	2.56
1989	3337439	55.52	41.48	3.01
1990	3411513	55.52	41.30	3.18
1991	3559487	56.00	40.61	3.38
1992	3736162	55.23	40.96	3.81
1993	3847821	54.71	40.15	5.14
1994	3831732	54.64	38.40	6.96
1995	3913824	53.21	39.22	7.58
1996	3928907	51.64	39.50	8.86
1997	4282130	46.66	44.06	9.28

Source: 'The Statistical Yearbook of Guangzhou 1998', p. 364.

Meanwhile, while the number and proportion of formal employees in publicly owned enterprises had declined, those in enterprises with other types of ownership had increased. Of the 2 million formal employees in 1997, about 1.26 million (63.03%) were employed in the state sector, 0.39 million (19.31%) in the collective sector, and over 0.35 million (17.66%) in enterprises with other types of ownership. Table 9.5 gives the distribution of formal employees in Guangzhou by types of ownership between 1982 and 1997.

Table 9.5: Distribution of formal employees by types of ownership in Guangzhou, 1982-97

Year	Total no. of formal employees	No. of formal employees State sector	Collective sector	Other ownership
1982	1792882	75.13	24.87	-
1983	1789569	75.71	24.29	-
1984	1819021	72.82	26.19	0.99
1985	1854461	73.65	24.93	1.42
1986	1911246	73.98	24.08	1.94
1987	1953812	74.26	23.27	2.46
1988	1879930	74.14	22.27	3.58
1989	1852865	73.75	21.39	4.86
1990	1893944	72.09	21.11	6.80
1991	1993914	69.80	22.02	8.17
1992	2063380	67.89	22.28	9.83
1993	2105320	65.79	22.49	11.72
1994	2093585	64.58	22.91	12.51
1995	2082361	63.82	21.39	14.79
1996	2028859	64.10	20.65	15.25
1997	1998075	63.03	19.31	17.66

Sources: 'The Statistical Yearbook of Guangzhou', various years.

Of the 1.26 million formal employees in the state sector in 1997, around 0.86 million were employed by the 4,425 SOEs, about 0.30 million by the 4,100 various public institutions, and around 0.10 million by the 1,158 government units (*The Statistical Yearbook of Guangzhou 1998*, p. 63). Of the 0.39 million formal employees in the collective sector, about 0.37 million were employed in the 19,428 collectively owned enterprises and the rest in various public institutions of collective ownership (*The Statistical Yearbook of Guangzhou 1998*, p. 75).

Reform of the Wage System

The wage system in Guangzhou started to reform in 1978, in response to the call of the central government to experiment the system of piecework wages and bonuses. Subsequently, the Guangdong provincial government began to design and issue specific regulations governing the implementation of the new wage system. Following the regulations of the provincial government, total bonuses that could be distributed by enterprises were fixed to range from 10 to 17 per cent of the total standard wage; a ceiling of 300 yuan was also set per worker per year. In enterprises where reforms such as 'self-responsibility for profits and losses', 'taxes replacing profits' and other economic responsibility systems had already been introduced, bonuses would come from 'bonus funds' derived from profits retained by enterprises.

The implementation of piecework wages and bonuses, together with the SOEs reforms, had given increasing autonomy to enterprises to design their own remuneration schemes, resulting in rapid diversification in the provision of wages and bonuses. For instance, by 1987, as many as 8 different types of wage systems had been developed by enterprises, and new schemes continued to be invented in the following years. By 1994, 746 enterprises in Guangzhou adopted the new wage system, with piecework wages and bonuses, involving over 70 per cent of the urban workers. The present wage system in Guangzhou is undoubtedly closely related to the economic efficiency of the enterprises and the performance of individual workers.

Table 9.6 gives the increase in wages in Guangzhou, as from 1985 to 1997. It shows that during this period, the average annual wage of formal employees in Guangzhou increased from 1,882 yuan to 13,611 yuan. In comparison with other major cities in China, the average wage of formal employees in Guangzhou has always been very high, or the highest in some years.

Table 9.6: Average wage of formal employees in Guangzhou, 1985-97 (yuan)

Year	Average wage	State-owned	Collectively owned	Others
1985	1596	1633	1474	1882
1986	1778	1823	1619	2119
1987	2008	2036	1882	2417
1988	2683	2733	2484	2896
1989	3272	3352	2869	3837
1990	3504	3597	3050	3955
1991	4022	4126	3531	4431
1992	4792	4979	4100	5060
1993	6342	6807	4987	6230
1994	8553	9386	6449	8636
1995	10317	11196	7644	10457
1996	11813	12868	8236	12280
1997	13118	14316	8768	13611

Sources: 'The Statistical Yearbook of Guangzhou', various years.

Another noteworthy point about the wage system in Guangzhou is that wages vary widely across enterprises with different types of ownership. In 1997, employees in the state sector received the highest average wage, at 14,316 yuan a year, and those in the collective sector received the lowest average wage, at 8,768 yuan a year. Within the state sector, the average wage was 15,636 yuan for formal employees in government units, 14,415 yuan for SOEs, and 13,593 yuan for public institutions (*The Statistical Yearbook of Guangzhou, 1998*, p. 49).

In summary, economic reforms have brought about drastic changes in both the employment and the wage systems in Guangzhou. First, unlike the past when almost everyone was employed in the state sector, nearly half of the urban employees in Guangzhou are now working in non-state enterprises. Second, economic reforms in Guangzhou have also wrecked, if not broken, the 'iron rice bowl', and workers understand that their wages are now directly related to their own performance. In short, the result of the economic reforms in Guangzhou represents no less than a dismantling of the SOEs, and together with it, a breakdown of the traditional protective network.

10 Old-age Pension System with Guangzhou Characteristics

Old-age pension reforms in Guangzhou have undergone two stages. In the first stage, spanning from 1983 to 1992, reforms were carried out on an incremental and limited basis. During this period, separate pension pools were established in enterprises according to types of ownership and the employment status of the employees, and were administered at either the municipal or district levels. The pension pools laid down different rates of contribution for participating enterprises, according to the types of ownership and employment status of the employees. Benefits were mainly related to the final standard wage and the length of service, but a variety of standards had been formulated to distribute benefits, resulting in substantial differences in the pension incomes of the retirees.

The second stage began in July 1993. The focus of the reforms in this stage has been to improve the administration of the pension schemes and the protective functions performed by them. Following the direction from the central government, separate pension pools were combined into a single unified municipal system with unified contribution rates and methods of providing benefits for all types of enterprises and employees. Since then, reform efforts have concentrated on making adjustments to the contribution rates, in the direction of increasing the contributions of individuals and decreasing that for enterprises, in accordance with the requirements of the central government. In 1998, the non-public sector was also brought into the old-age pension system.

The First Stage of Pension Reform: 1983-92

In the first stage of pension reform, the major efforts of the Guangzhou government were to convert traditional pension provisions and 'administration by individual enterprises' into pools across enterprises with the same type of ownership, and for workers of the same employment status. As a result, six separate pension pools were established. In chronological order of implementation, pools were established to cover contract workers in SOEs in 1983, permanent workers in SOEs in 1985, workers in the labour service companies in 1986, employees in municipal collectively owned enterprises in 1988, temporary workers with urban household registration in 1989, and employees in district/street collectively owned enterprises in 1990. In 1987, domestic employees in foreign-funded enterprises were also brought into the pools according to the employees' employment status.

Until August 1993, enterprise contributions were set at 21.5 per cent of the wage bill for permanent workers in SOEs, 23.5 per cent for permanent workers in collectively owned enterprises, and 15 per cent for contract workers and temporary workers. Permanent workers in SOEs and collectively owned enterprises did not have to make individual contributions until July 1992, while contract workers and temporary workers contributed 2 per cent of their wages. Two different systems were in operation to finance the pension benefits: The pools for contract and temporary workers were fully funded as there were no retirees when the pools were first established. Pools for permanent workers in SOEs and collectively owned enterprises were operated largely on a pay-as-you-go basis and the contribution rates were determined mainly by the costs of pension obligations. Funds in the two systems were managed separately, and they could not be used for adjustment between pools.

Contract Workers

The reform of the pension system in Guangzhou started with the implementation of a contributory pension scheme designed in 1983 for contract workers. It was only natural and convenient to begin with the contract workers because, unlike permanent workers in the SOEs and the collectively owned enterprises whose pension systems were both sophisticated and deeply rooted, contract workers were newly recruited and they did not have a pension system of their own. Hence, pension arrangements for contract workers were a piece of blank paper, where trial or experimental schemes could easily be implemented.

The initial scheme designed for contract workers was a combination of arrangements for providing benefits during their years of employment and for retirement protection, known as 'double insurance' system. The scheme contained the following features:

1. Enterprises are responsible for providing welfare for contract workers in the years of employment in the same way as they are doing to permanent workers.
2. Pooling covers five items of benefits in the course of retirement, including pensions, living subsidies, death and funeral allowances, and survivors' benefits as specified in government regulations.
3. Enterprises and workers both contribute to the pool. Enterprises

contribute 15 per cent of the total wages of contract workers, and contract workers contribute 2 per cent of the wage.
4. The Labour Service Company is responsible for managing the pool.

After 1984, social insurance companies were established at both the municipal and district levels. The social insurance companies became responsible for managing pension pools in place of the Labour Service Company. They were charged with the responsibility of designing pension pools for SOEs, managing the pool for contract workers, providing instructions for collectively owned enterprises to design their own pension pools, and conducting research on pensions for temporary workers, self-employed workers and domestic workers in joint ventures.

At the end ɔf 1988, nearly all contract workers in the urban areas were brought into the pool. By 1992, the pool covered 139,000 workers, but only 45 retirees were receiving their benefits.

Permanent Workers in SOEs

The earliest pool for SOEs was established in October 1985. The pool was exclusively funded by participating enterprises, with the contribution rate set at 14 per cent of the total wages of permanent workers plus the existing pension costs. Workers did not have to make individual contributions. Initially, the pool covered only three items of benefits, including pensions, subsidies for grain and non-staple food, and living allowances. In 1988, the scope of benefits was expanded to cover thirteen items. New items included invalidity and disability payment, survivors' compensations and various new categories of subsidies as specified in government regulations. Together with the increases in benefit items and the number of retirees, contribution rates were raised in July 1988 from 14 per cent to 21.5 per cent of the wage bill plus existing pension costs. By the end of 1991, the pool covered 450,000 workers and over 190,000 retirees.

Starting from July 1992, permanent workers in SOEs, municipal collectively owned enterprises and foreign-funded enterprises in Guangzhou were required to make an individual contribution of 3.5 yuan per person per month, in response to the requirements stated in State Council Document 33 of 1991. Social insurance companies at different levels were responsible for collecting the funds and delivering the pensions. By the end of 1992, the number of formal employees covered by the pool decreased from 450,000 in the previous year to 438,000, while that of retirees increased from 190,000 to 207,000. The decline in the number of covered employees was mainly due to the fact that formal employees began to shift to the non-public sector.

Employees in Labour Service Companies

Labour service companies were established during the early 1980s. Their main purpose was to provide employment opportunities for workers, who were known as 'young people waiting for employment'. The design of the pension pool for employees in the labour service companies in 1986 was quite similar to that for contract workers:

1. Social insurance companies at different levels are responsible for collecting funds and delivering benefits. They are responsible for managing the pool for municipal labour service companies and units of the central government, the provincial government, and the army stationed in Guangzhou.
2. Enterprises contribute 15 per cent of the wage bill, and workers individually contribute 2 per cent of their wage. Contributions are made on a monthly basis.
3. Benefits cover pensions, food subsidies, medical fees and death and funeral benefits. The provision of pensions is linked to the length of contribution years and the standard wage. A worker who reaches retirement age after contributing for 15 years gets 60 per cent of the standard wage. If a worker's length of contribution is more than 15 years, he or she can get an additional 1 per cent of the standard wage for each of the additional contribution years. Workers with 10 to 15 contribution years get 40 per cent of the standard wage. Those who contributed for less than 10 years will get a lump-sum payment according to the length of contribution years.

Municipal Collectively Owned Enterprises

In August 1988, the Guangzhou government issued 'Temporary Regulations on the Pension Pool for Municipal Collectively Owned Enterprises and Institutions', specifying the coverage of the pool, items of benefits to be pooled, contribution rates, standards of benefits and the management of the pool. The Guangzhou Labour Department and the People's Bank of China (Guangzhou Branch) would jointly design specific measures to implement the regulations. The design of the pool is as follows:

1. The coverage of the pool includes permanent workers in municipal collectively owned enterprises which maintain separate accounting units, permanent workers in municipal collective owned labour service companies, and domestic permanent workers of collective ownership in joint ventures and foreign-funded enterprises.
2. Funds are to be raised according to the principle of 'expenditure plus small reserves'. Enterprises contribute 23.5 per cent of the total wages of permanent workers plus total existing pension costs.
3. Qualifications for retirement and standards of benefits will be in accordance with relevant government regulations.
4. The Guangzhou Social Insurance Company is responsible for the unified management of the funds. 5 per cent of the funds is to be kept as reserves, another 0.5 per cent to be drawn by the agency as administrative expenses.

By the end of 1992, the pool covered 443 municipal collectively owned enterprises and institutions, 106,000 workers and 56,000 retirees. From July 1992, workers were required to make an individual contribution of 3.5 yuan per person per month in accordance with the regulations of the State Council Document 33 of 1991.

Temporary Workers

In October 1989, to implement 'Regulations on Pensions for Temporary Workers' issued by the Guangdong Province, the Labour Department in Guangzhou developed the following measures to be carried out for temporary workers working in the city:

1. The pool is to cover, in the beginning, temporary workers in all types of enterprises, organizations, public institutions and government units in Guangzhou, who are permanent residents in either urban or rural areas of Guangzhou. Coverage will gradually be extended to include all non-permanent residents.
2. The pool for temporary workers with urban household registration should be designed in the same way as that for contract workers. Pension schemes based on savings, instead of social pooling, are to be set up for temporary workers with rural household registration. When workers retire, benefits will be provided in lump-sum payments equivalent to the total sum of contributions made by enterprises and individual employees plus interests minus administrative expenses.
3. Social insurance companies at different levels are responsible for

collecting funds and delivering benefits.

At the end of 1992, the pool covered 40,000 temporary workers and only 29 retirees had received their pensions in the form of lump-sum payments.

District / Street Collectively Owned Enterprises

Pension reforms in district/street collectively owned enterprises began as early as in 1983, largely because these enterprises never had a sound pension system. In 'Temporary Regulations on the Retirement and Resignation of Workers and Temporary Regulations on the Arrangement of Old, Weak, Sick and Disabled Cadres' of 1978, the State Council recommended that these district/street enterprises should design their own pension systems after considering their own individual situations. Because of this, pension schemes for district/street enterprises differed widely, particularly with regard to standards of benefits and the form of administration.

Among the various types of enterprises, district/street collectively own enterprises had the most frequent difficulties in delivering retirement benefits. Unlike employees in SOEs and municipal collectively owned enterprises, who were assured, in different degrees, by the government to receive their benefits after retirement, workers in district/street collectively owned enterprises seldom had regular incomes after their retirement. It was therefore an urgent matter to protect the retirement of the employees in district/street collectively owned enterprises.

Beginning from 1983, pension pools for district/street collectively owned enterprises began to be set up in some counties and districts of Guangzhou. Separate pools were also established for certain district/street industrial or specialized companies, with uniform contribution rates. In 1990, the Guangzhou government issued 'Trial Measures for Pension Pooling for Employees in District/Street Collectively Owned Enterprises', with the following guidelines:

1. Social pooling is to be effected at the district level, covering permanent workers in collectively owned enterprises managed by district/street administrations, including enterprises on contractual, leasing or joint operation arrangements, joint ventures, and public institutions not financed by government allocations.
2. The pension system is to be established with two tiers of benefits: a statutory basic benefit and a supplementary benefit provided

voluntarily by enterprises in accordance with their own individual situations.

3. Retirement ages are 60 for men and 55 for women, who have contributed for 15 years. Flexibility is provided for invalid or disabled workers.
4. The basic pension covers 35 per cent of the average local wage of employees in collectively owned enterprises in the urban areas in the year when the worker retires. The supplementary pension is linked to the length of contribution and the final standard wage: 1 per cent of the standard wage for each year of contribution.
5. The Guangzhou government recommended that enterprises should adopt the same contribution rates. The base for calculating contributions by the municipal collectively owned enterprises should be 23.5 per cent of the wage bill plus the costs of existing pensions; workers should make an individual contribution of 2 per cent of their wage on a monthly basis. Flexible contribution methods are proposed for enterprises to adopt, according to their own actual conditions.
6. District social insurance companies are responsible for collecting funds and delivering benefits through unified funds management. Adjustment funds should be kept at the district level. If the contributions of an enterprise are less than its pension obligations, 70 per cent of the difference is to be covered by the district fund and 30 per cent by the pool of the municipal collectively owned enterprises.
7. District social insurance companies or the enterprises themselves can manage either the supplementary pension scheme. District fund and the municipal pool will not be used to cover deficits in the costs of paying supplementary pensions.
8. District social insurance companies keep 5 per cent of the funds as reserves, which will be used as adjustment funds across the district, and 1 per cent would be deducted as administrative expenses.

At the end of 1992, the pool covered 41,973 workers and 46,911 retirees. Together with the unification of management of the separate pension schemes in 1993, funds management responsibility was transferred to the social insurance companies, which can use the funds for adjustment purposes. Starting from January 1994, the method of providing the basic benefits was unified, with social insurance companies gradually responsible for all the district funds.

The pension reforms that took place in Guangzhou, from 1983 to 1992, looked rather chaotic and difficult to follow. The reforms have, however, enabled Guangzhou to develop some special features of its own.

First, new pension schemes were often first experimented in

Guangzhou, such as the one for contract workers, before the central government had perceived the need to pass the appropriate regulations for the entire country. As a result, the pension schemes in Guangzhou had often features different from the national standards.

Second, the greater variations that existed between the various pension schemes for different types of employees in Guangzhou were the result of the fact that Guangzhou was the first city in China to have adopted a market economy. Enterprises in Guangzhou were thus allowed to devise their own schemes in accordance with their own situations. Hence, while enterprises in Guangzhou were required to comply with the national standards, they had also retained special features of their own.

Third, up to the end of 1992, the pension system that had been developed in Guangzhou was one of the most advanced in the country. Pension reforms in Guangzhou were also known to be realistic, as no attempts had been made to introduce schemes that could not be implemented. However, it is worthy to note that, same as other cities, coverage for old-age pensions in Guangzhou, at the end of this stage, was still largely confined to employees in the state sector.

The Second Stage of Pension Reform: 1993-

By 1992, pension pools in Guangzhou covered most of the enterprises and workers except migrant workers and those in the non-public sector. However, as mentioned before, the existence of separate pools according to the different types of ownership and employment status has produced a highly fragmented pension system in Guangzhou. In addition to the six separate enterprise pension pools, eleven sectors, like railway, telecommunications, water conservancy, had established their own pension pools.

The control over the formulation of pension policies and the administration of the various schemes was also widely dispersed among different government departments. While the Labour Department was responsible for administering the pension pools for urban enterprises, the Personnel Department was in charge of pensions for employees of government units and public institutions. The Civil Affairs Department was responsible for implementing social welfare programmes as well as the pension schemes in the nearby rural areas. In addition, the administration of pension pools for units of the central and provincial governments and the army stationed in Guangzhou belonged to the responsibility of the provincial social insurance bureau. In many instances, the Planning Commission, the Finance Department, the Systems Reform Commission, and the banks also contributed in different ways to the design and implementation of the various pension schemes.

The Shortcomings of the Pension Pools

No doubt, the wide dispersion of authority over pension policy and administration has produced a fragmented pension system in Guangzhou. The separate pooling for different types of enterprises and employees could, however, be regarded as a reflection of the diversity of the city's economy and the complexity of the labour system that had emerged since the economic reforms. Indeed, in the course of transiting from a planned economy to a socialist market economy, enterprises of various types of ownership would emerge and exist simultaneously. Within individual enterprises, workers of different employment status would also appear and must be treated differently in terms of their wage and retirement benefits. The wide diversification of the economy and the high degree of differentiation in the labour system appeared, thus, to be inevitable and the differences would naturally lead to the establishment of separate pension pools.

While separate pools might be necessary, they have also created a number of problems.

First, varied contribution rates and payment standards within the same enterprise had proved to be a heavy burden for both the enterprises and social insurance agencies responsible for administering and managing the pools. Efficiency was lost as a result, notwithstanding the creation of social insurance agencies at both the municipal and district levels.

Second, different contribution rates and benefit standards within the same enterprise had been perceived to be socially inequitable, especially when retirement benefits were related to the year of employment and the final standard wage of the retirees. Hence, retirees with different final standard wages would get widely different levels of retirement benefits, and the resulting gaps in retirement benefits might also be very substantial between individuals working in different enterprises. In 1993, the average pension for retirees in municipal collectively owned enterprises was 230 yuan, while that for retirees in district/street collectively owned enterprises was only 170 yuan. In other words, pensions were primarily distributed as compensations for past services and were not related to the needs of the retirees. Consequently, the function of the old-age pensions as a mechanism to protect the general living standards of the retirees had often been queried.

Third, retirement benefits were generally low, and were insufficient at times for retirees to maintain an adequate level of living. In 1993, average pension for retirees in municipal collectively owned enterprises was 230 yuan, 44 per cent of the municipal average wage at 522 yuan, and 59.7 per cent of the per capita average living expenditure at 385.4 yuan. The situation was worse for retirees in district/street collectively owned enterprises at 170 yuan, 33 per cent of the district/street average wage and 44 per cent of the per capital average living expenditure.

Finally, diversity of pension standards and fragmentation in administration limited the capacity for pension pools to spread risks through unified fund adjustment. Pension pools, operated separately at municipal and district levels, for different sectors, and across enterprises and workers with different types of ownership, were neither able to solve the problem of inequality in enterprise pension burdens, nor were they able to provide reliable insurance for retirees. In the state and collectively owned enterprises where pension obligations were generally heavier, they might experience delays in pension payments when individual enterprises failed to pay their contributions in time.

The 'Four-Unification'

In 1992, the Ministry of Labour of the central government drafted a proposal to reform the method of providing pension benefits, inviting suggestions from local governments. In response to the pension reform proposal of the Ministry of Labour, the Guangzhou government and concerned departments designed in 1993 a series of measures to reform the pension system in Guangzhou. The new policies followed the 'four-unification' proposed, namely: unified funds management, unified contribution rates for all types of enterprises and workers, unified method of providing pension benefits, and unified adjustment funds.

The unification of funds management came first. Beginning July 1993, the previous method of fund collection and pension delivery according to types of ownership and employment status was changed into unified management based on the type of industries or sectors, while keeping separate accounts for permanent workers, contract workers and temporary workers. Meanwhile, social insurance companies restructured their management into three pension departments. Department one was in charge of pooling for the municipal industrial sector; department two for other municipal units that were not covered by department one; department three for units under the jurisdiction of the central government, the provincial government, the army and other localities located in Guangzhou. The last one was also in charge of pooling for foreign-funded enterprises, private enterprises, and self-employed commercial and industrial households and their employees. As a result, employees of the same enterprise would come under the administration of one single department within the social insurance companies instead of being assigned, as in the past, to different schemes according to their employment status.

Second, contribution rates were unified for all types of enterprises and workers. Starting from August 1993, enterprises contributed 24.5 per cent of the wage bill for all types of workers plus the costs of pensions for the existing retirees. All employees, on the other hand, were required to make individual contributions of 2 per cent of the wage, which was to be increased along with economic growth. The Labour Department of Guangzhou defined the wage base for contribution as the sum of the standard wage plus various subsidies and bonuses as listed on the payrolls of the employees. Wages in excess of two times of the average local wage were not liable for contribution, while workers whose earnings were 60 per cent below the average local wage contributed 60 per cent of the average local wage. Owners and managers of private enterprises and individual commercial/ industrial households in the urban areas were responsible for paying both their own contributions and that of their employees. With the unification of the management of the pension funds, social insurance companies could then make the necessary adjustments at the municipal level.

Third, the methods of providing benefits were reformed. The basic benefits consisted of a basic pension and a supplementary pension. The basic pension was related to the average local wage prior to the retirement year and the number of contribution years. A retiree received 25 per cent of the average local wage if he or she had contributed for 15 years or above, and 20 per cent for 10 to 15 years. Cadres under the privileged retirement arrangement would get 30 per cent of the average local wage.

The supplementary pension was related to a worker's indexed average wage during the contribution years as well as the number of contribution years. A retiree received 1.3 per cent of the indexed average wage for each contribution year if he or she had contributed for 10 years or above. For those whose length of contribution was less than 10 years, they would get a lump sum equivalent to two months' indexed average wage for each year of contribution. A worker's officially recorded service years prior to the implementation of this method could be counted as contribution years in calculating benefits.

The new method of providing benefits began to take effect from October 1993 for municipal SOEs, municipal collectively owned enterprises, foreign-funded enterprises, private enterprises, enterprises under joint operation, stockholding enterprises, and individual proprietors, and from January 1994 for county and county-level city enterprises and district/street collectively owned enterprises.

Finally, pension funds were pooled for unified adjustment across the municipality. Social insurance companies were put in charge of the funds and could use them through unified adjustment for all participating enterprises or their employees. Thus, a partially funded system based on the principle of 'financing according to expenditure plus small surpluses and partial accumulation', as recommended by the State Council in Document 33 of 1991, was established.

Special arrangements were made for workers who retired in the three years following the implementation of the new method. Higher standards would be applied to these retirees after calculating and comparing their levels of benefits before and after the implementation of the new method. If the benefits under the new method were higher than benefits under the old one, a ceiling for the increase was set at 10 per cent of the old benefits. The new method did not apply to retirees who retired prior to its implementation. Benefits for these retirees were to be adjusted every year on July 1, and the adjustment would be made based on increases in the average local wage or in the price index or according to state regulations.

The New Pension Scheme

Since the unification of the separate pension schemes into a single municipal system in 1993, three major adjustments were made in the contribution rates. In 1995, the contribution rate of enterprises was reduced from 24.5 to 24 per cent of the wage bill plus the costs of existing pensions; contribution rate of employees was increased from 2 to 3 per cent of the wage. This adjustment was made in response to the State Council Document 6 of 1995, which recommended that local governments should gradually increase the contribution rate of employees and decrease that for enterprises.

In 1997, a second adjustment in contribution rates was made in accordance with the State Council Document 26, which set a floor of 4 per cent of the wage for individual contribution and a ceiling of 20 per cent of the wage bill for enterprise contribution for 1997. Accordingly, the contribution rate of enterprises was further reduced to 23 per cent of the wage bill plus pension costs, while that of employees increased to 4 per cent.

The third adjustment in contribution rates was made in 1998, which brought the contribution rate of enterprises closer to that required by the central government in the State Council Document 26 of 1997. The contribution rate for enterprises changed from 23 per cent of the wage bill plus pension costs to 23 per cent of the wage bill alone, while the individual contribution rate was raised to 5 per cent of the wage. This readjustment reduced the revenues of the pension funds by 6.5 per cent. The decreases in funds would be covered by the reserves, with the government being the last resort for pension deficits. A three-year period was set for the enterprise contribution rate to be reduced to the 20 per cent level of the wage bill required by the central government.

In April 1998, the Guangzhou government formulated new measures to bring the non-public sector into the municipal pension system, which began to take effect as from August 1998. Following the stipulations in the State Council Document 6 of 1995 and Document 26 of 1997, the design of the new pension system would involve both social pooling and the setting-up of individual accounts. Under the new arrangement, owners of all enterprises would contribute 19 per cent of the average local wage, of which 11 per cent to be recorded into individual accounts and 8 per cent into the social pool. Employees would contribute 8 per cent of their wage. A minimum sum of contribution was set at 40 per cent of the average local wage.

Benefits would include a basic pension equivalent to 20 per cent of the average local wage, to be paid out of the social pool for retirees who had contributed for 15 years and above. The individual account pension would be equivalent to the total sum accumulated in the account divided by 120. Those with less than 15 years of contribution would not be eligible for the basic pension paid out of the social pool; their individual account pension would, however, be paid in a lump sum when they reached the retirement age.

Before the introduction of the new pension system, as mentioned before, attempts had already been made to bring the non-public sector into the coverage of the municipal pension system as early as in 1993. In 'Regulations on Social Insurance of Enterprise Employees' issued by the Guangzhou government in 1993, owners and employees in private enterprises and individual commercial/industrial households were required to participate in the then pension scheme. However, the implementation of the regulations proved to be difficult, as owners and employees in private enterprises were not as organized as those were in the state sector.

Towards the end of the 1990s, the Guangzhou government increasingly realized that the participation of the non-public sector, which had rapidly expanded, would be crucial to the future development of the pension system, as well as increasing the source of financing. Being determined to extend the coverage of the pension system to cover the non-public sector, the Guangzhou government made special arrangements to accompany the 1998 design. One of the attempts was to set up the Industrial and Commercial Administration Department, charged with the task to provide information to the Social Insurance Funds Management Centre about new entries in the private or individual business sector, so that they could collect the appropriate pension funds.

At the end of 1997, the municipal pension system of Guangzhou covered about 600,000 employees and 370,000 retirees (Table 10.1). The pension coverage was still very limited, as those covered represented only 35 per cent of the formal employees, or 29 per cent of the urban employees. One reason for the limited coverage was that the number of formal employees in the state sector had declined in the 1990s, while that of urban employees and retirees had kept increasing. In other words, unless employees in the non-state sector could gradually be brought into the pension system under the new arrangements, a substantial number of retirees in Guangzhou would be left unprotected in the coming years.

Table 10.1: Coverage of pension scheme in Guangzhou, 1993-97 (persons)

Year	Urban Employees	Formal employees	Covered employees	Covered retirees
1993	2302914	2105320	630000	310000
1994	2360367	2093585	636400	319600
1995	2378885	2082361	723000	367100
1996	2377076	2028859	1100000	354900
1997	2395375	1998075	705555	386100

Sources: 'The Guangzhou Yearbook', various years.

Problems with Recent Reforms

After more than two decades of reform, the pension system in Guangzhou has no doubt achieved some successes. As mentioned before, during the first stage of reform from 1983 to 1992, the pension system in Guangzhou had been unified at the municipal level, instead of having the responsibility falling on individual enterprises. However, towards the end of the 1990s, even after the introduction of new measures in 1997, the pension system in Guangzhou still remained inadequate and suffered, at least, in two main areas: Partial coverage and ineffective enforcement.

At the end of 1997, Guangzhou had a total number of 2.4 million urban employees, about 2 million of them were formal employees. Among the formal employees, around 1.58 million worked in enterprises, 0.32

million in public institutions and 0.1 million in governmental organizations. Of the 1.58 million formal employees in enterprises, 0.86 million worked in SOEs, 0.37 million were employed by collectively owned enterprises and 0.35 million in enterprises with other types of ownership (*The Statistical Yearbook of Guangzhou, 1998*). The pension system, however, only covered 706,000 formal employees and 386,000 retirees (including about 30,000 retirees from public institutions and governmental organizations). In terms of the 1.58 million formal employees in enterprises, who are the targets of pension reforms, the pension system covered 44.68 per cent. Compared with the 2.4 million urban employees, the coverage was even lower, at less than one third of the active urban labour force.

Up to the end of the 1990s, the pension system in Guangzhou covered mainly enterprises with public ownership, particularly SOEs and municipal collectively owned enterprises, which were still under the effective control of the government. At the end of 1997, the number of formal employees in SOEs and collectively owned enterprises was about 1.23 million, of which only 706,000 employees (57.5%) participated in the pension scheme. Enterprises or employees that were not covered by the pension system were often those for which governmental control was very limited. Even within the public sector, enterprises that were loosely subordinated to SOEs or municipal collectively owned enterprises were often left out. Most of these enterprises were registered as collectively owned enterprises, but were actually operated like private enterprises, and it was estimated that they employed around 200,000 urban employees. As for the private sector, which included private enterprises and self-employed commercial/industrial households, it accounted for over 500,000 owners and 735,000 employees and they were generally not included in the coverage. It is disappointing that two decades of pension reforms in Guangzhou have only achieved partial coverage.

It should be noted at this juncture that the number of enterprise retirees has been increasing at around 10,000 persons a year, when the number of employees in the public ownership sector has been declining. In July 1998, the number of covered enterprise employees decreased further to around 600,000, while that of retirees increased to over 370,000, the ratio of contributors to retirees being 1.68 : 1, the highest in China. In the last few years of the 1990s, the monthly revenue and expenditure of the pension funds stood around 170 million and 155 million respectively. It was estimated that at this rate, the annual reserves of all social insurance funds would be insufficient to pay one month's pension of all current retirees.

In addition, the social insurance funds were accumulated to cover also the benefits of retirees whose employers had declared bankrupt or run into financial difficulties. Between 1990 and 1994, enterprises with financial difficulties were allowed to delay to make contributions, and social insurance companies had to use the reserve funds to provide pensions for the retirees of these enterprises. Since 1995, enterprises declaring bankrupt had to turn over to social insurance companies a sum equal to five years of pension costs and the medical fees of their retirees. After the five years, retirees would be cut off from their enterprises, and the Retiree Administration Office, which was established under the direct jurisdiction of the Guangzhou government, would step in to take over the responsibility of looking after them, including delivering pensions and reimbursing medical fees. In 1997, there were about 5,000 retirees that were covered under this arrangement, with their pensions coming from the reserved funds. With the number of pensioners increasing and that of contributors decreasing, the current pay-as-you-go system will eventually be dried up. In order to maintain the solvency of the current pension system, it is most essential for employees in the non-public sector to be brought into the pension pool.

Implementation of the new pension system has also proved to be difficult. In 1996, the Social Insurance Administration Bureau was established, responsible for designing, administering and coordinating the implementation of all social insurance programmes, including old-age pensions, unemployment, industrial accidents, medical care and childbearing. Meanwhile, social insurance companies were renamed Social Insurance Finance and Management Centres and were put under the Labour Department. The establishment of the two new organizations has, however, made little progress in expanding the funding base. Relatively high contribution rates, economic difficulties encountered by enterprises, and the lack of legal support for policy implementation, have in combination led to continued decline in the compliance rate. When enterprises or individuals delayed or refused to make contributions, the Social Insurance Administration Bureau and the Social Insurance Finance and Management Centre could in fact do little except persuading. It was reported that this situation has brought to the attention of the State Council.

In short, despite some of the successes achieved during the second stage of reform, the pension system in Guangzhou still suffered from limited coverage and ineffective enforcement.

11 New Ventures in Unemployment, Injuries and Death, and Maternity Insurance

Unemployment and Laid-off Formal Employees in Guangzhou

Since the mid-1990s, changes in the labour and wage system, in combination with the reform of the SOEs, have resulted in a rising trend of unemployment in Guangzhou. From 1985 to 1997, the number of unemployed formal employees in Guangzhou increased from 36,000 to 65,000 persons, although the unemployment rate remained within 3 per cent of the total number of formal employees. However, as SOEs and collectively owned enterprises increasingly found it difficult to absorb the unemployed, the only way to keep the unemployment rate was to expand employment opportunities in the non-state sector and to encourage workers to become self-employed. Table 11.1 gives the picture of unemployment and re-employment in Guangzhou between the 1985 and 1997.

Table 11.1: Unemployment in Guangzhou, 1985-97 (persons)

Year	No. of unemployed	
	Beginning of year	End of year
1985	114924	35561
1990	154869	56542
1995	137146	63495
1996	141184	56037
1997	120945	65339

Source: 'The Statistical Yearbook of Guangzhou 1998', p. 88.

Since unemployment statistics in Guangzhou included only those who reported to and were registered with the Labour Department as unemployed and were receiving unemployment benefits, the above figures could hardly reflect the real situation of unemployment. It was known that a considerable number of the unemployed did not register with the Labour Department, especially when they thought they would soon be able to find a job. Besides, the unemployment statistics did not include the laid-off formal employees. It has been mentioned that the number of laid-off formal employees in Guangzhou rapidly increased in the latter part of the 1990s, with the official figures rising from 10,000 in 1995 to 60,000 in 1996, six times within a short period of one year. At the end of 1997, the number of laid-off formal employees declined to 53,400, which was about 2.7 per cent of the formal employees in Guangzhou.

Among the 53,400 laid-off formal employees at the end of 1997, enterprises alone displaced 51,700 employees, amounting to 3.28 per cent of employees in enterprises. If the number of laid-off formal employees were counted as the unemployed, the unemployment rate in Guangzhou should be much higher. Moreover, the percentage of surplus workers in Guangzhou was estimated at about 8 to 10 per cent. Although the figure was much lower than the 30 per cent national average, it was by no means a small number. In terms of the 2,405,600 active urban labour force at the end of 1996, the number of surplus workers was around 192,500 to 240,600, and they were the potential laid-off formal employees in future years.

Implementation of Unemployment Insurance

Unemployment insurance started in Guangzhou in 1987 in response to the stipulations of the State Council Document 77 of 1986, which laid down the requirement for SOEs to establish unemployment insurance for their workers. Based on the 1986 regulations, unemployment insurance was established in Guangzhou in 1987. Sources of funding included contributions from enterprises, bank interests accrued to the funds, and government subsidies. A contribution rate of 1 per cent of the total standard wage was set for participating enterprises. The pool covered all types of workers in SOEs, contract workers in government organs, public institutions and mass organizations, and domestic workers in foreign-funded enterprises.

Unemployment insurance benefits were provided according to the length of service and the standard wage, with the duration ranging from 6 to 24 months for workers with at least 1 year of service. An unemployed worker with over 5 years of service could receive benefits for a maximum period of 24 months. For them, benefits during the first 12 months ranged from 60 to 75 per cent of the standard wage, depending on the length of service, and 50 per cent during the next 12 months. Workers with 3 to less than 5 years of service would receive 60 per cent of the standard wage for a maximum period of 12 months, and those with 1 to less than 3 years of service would get 60 per cent of the standard wage for a maximum period of 6 months. Unemployed workers with less than 1 year of service were not eligible for benefits. A floor of 35 yuan and a ceiling of 100 yuan per month were set for the benefits. Unemployed workers who were dismissed by enterprises due to violation of regulations would receive benefits at a reduced rate. Domestic workers in foreign-funded enterprises could get 55 per cent of the average wage of the two years prior to unemployment if the enterprises had not adopted the local wage system.

Medical fees for the unemployed were separately delivered in fixed amounts. Unemployed workers with less than 15 years of service could get 5 yuan of medical fees per month, and 7 yuan with over 15 years of service. The Labour Service Company was charged with the responsibility of collecting and managing the funds, while district/street labour service companies were responsible for delivering benefits.

In the following years, the coverage of the scheme continued to expand. In the beginning, coverage was restricted mainly to permanent workers who lost jobs due to reform of enterprises, and contract workers whose labour contracts were terminated in a normal way. In 1991, employees eligible for benefits were expanded to include contract workers whose labour contract was terminated either voluntarily or by enterprises due to economic factors, and surplus workers dismissed by enterprises as a result of regrouping of labour. In 1993, workers in collectively owned enterprises were brought into the coverage of unemployment insurance by contributing 1 yuan for each employee per month.

In 1994, in response to the State Council's 'Regulations on Unemployment Insurance for Employees in SOEs' (Document 110 of 1993), the Guangzhou government issued 'Regulations on Unemployment Insurance for Employees in Guangzhou'. The regulations extended the coverage to all workers whose labour relations were cut off from their enterprises, and readjusted the unemployment benefits by relating them to length of service and the average local wage instead of the standard wage. All unemployed workers with at least 1 year of service were made to qualify for unemployment benefits. The duration of benefits ranged from 3 to 24 months, depending on the length of service. Unemployment benefits were further divided into three levels. Unemployed workers with over 1 year of service were eligible for unemployment benefits and medical fees for at least 3 months. Providing 1 month's benefits for each 6 months of service, with 24 months being the maximum duration would compensate additional length of service. Workers dismissed by enterprises due to violation of regulations or whose labour contracts terminated voluntarily ahead of time could receive benefits for a maximum period of 12 months. Compensated service years would not be counted in the calculation of unemployment benefits for workers becoming re-unemployed.

Starting from 1995, unemployment benefits were made to relate with both the average local wage and the length of service. During the first 12 months of unemployment, unemployed workers would get 35 per cent of the average local wage if they had 1 to 6 years of service, 40 per cent with 7 to 10 years of service, and 45 per cent if the length of service was over 11 years. For the remaining months, all unemployed got 35 per cent of the average local wage. In addition, unemployed workers with 10 years of service were provided with 10 yuan of medical fees per month. With more than 10 years of service, the amount of medical fees would be increased for 1 yuan for each additional year of service. Disabled unemployed contract workers got 20 yuan of medical fees per month, with an increase of 2 yuan for each service year above 11 years of service. Unemployed workers receiving treatment in hospital could apply for a reimbursement of 50 to 70 per cent of the expenses from the unemployment insurance agency where their households were registered. Meanwhile, the contribution rate of enterprises was changed to 0.7 per cent of the average local wage. Apart from providing unemployment benefits, medical fees, and other related expenses for the unemployed, 20 per cent of the funds would be used for providing training and financial support for the unemployed to re-start economic activities, and 8 per cent for administrative expenses. At the end of 1997, around one third of urban employees in Guangzhou were covered under the system. Table 11.2 shows the situation of unemployment insurance in Guangzhou as at 1997.

Table 11.2: Unemployment insurance in Guangzhou, 1987-97 (persons)

Year	Urban employees	Covered employees	Beneficiaries
1987	2043346	–	530
1988	1965365	840000	3057
1989	1953167	890000	2242
1990	2002552	–	–
1991	2114056	903500	72227
1992	2205681	925000	14600
1993	2302914	–	–
1994	2360367	1200000	27513
1995	2378885	890000	–
1996	2377076	930000	–
1997	2395375	875400	310000

Sources: 'The Guangzhou Yearbook', various years.
–: Information not available.

Measures to Support Laid-off Employees and to Promote Employment

In the early years of economic reforms, rapid economic growth provided a relatively favourable employment environment for Guangzhou. Foreign-funded ventures, service industries, private enterprises, and self-employed workers increased rapidly in number, absorbing a considerable proportion of surplus workers from SOEs. However, the number of surplus workers in Guangzhou began to grow drastically as from the mid-1990s.

Over the years, the Guangzhou government has developed four measures to support the laid-off formal employees, based on relevant regulations of the central government.

The most important measure was the development of a variety of employment promotion programmes, with preferential policies being designed to support surplus workers to begin their own economic activities or to get re-employed through their own efforts. Enterprises were also encouraged to provide multiple channels to absorb the surplus workers.

Second, adjustments were made in labour policy to control and limit the in coming of non-local workers.

Third, various programmes were implemented to provide support for laid-off formal employees, including the establishment of re-employment funds and re-employment service centres and stations.

Finally, policies were developed to protect the basic living of laid-off formal employees.

In addition to the support for laid-off employees, the Guangzhou government had started to deal with the problem of surplus workers long before it was recognized as a problem by the central government. In 1989, the Guangzhou government issued 'Temporary Regulations on Surplus Workers in SOEs', which established the policy of helping the surplus workers through the joint efforts of both the enterprises and the society as a whole. Surplus workers were defined in the document as 'workers forced to leave their jobs due to changes in production and management, or regrouping of labour'.

However, the regulations applied only to permanent workers. For surplus contract and temporary workers, enterprises were allowed to terminate their employment whenever necessary. As for the permanent workers, enterprises had the primary responsibility of helping the surplus workers, though it was hoped that the responsibility would eventually be transferred to the society when circumstances allowed. In actual practice, enterprises were required to provide employment opportunities for surplus workers by setting up new economic units that would have separate accounting and must be responsible for their own losses. Furthermore, training programmes would be organized for the surplus workers to help them to get re-employed. Surplus workers would also be encouraged to seek new employment or to be self-employed.

The regulations also provided incentives for enterprises or labour service companies to employ surplus or laid-off formal employees. If the number of re-employed laid-off formal employees reached over 60 per cent of the total labour force in an enterprise or labour service company, a two-year tax exemption would be applied, subject to the approval of the fiscal and taxation departments. Other tax preferences would also be available for these enterprises when they encountered financial difficulties.

In 1994, the Guangzhou government issued 'Temporary Regulations on the Arrangement for Workers in Enterprises under Organizational Transformation'. The regulations reaffirmed the policy of helping the laid-off formal employees through the joint efforts of the enterprises and concerned departments, and that more incentives should be provided to promote re-employment of laid-off formal employees. The regulations stated that laid-off and surplus employees would be given further preferences in receiving labour services such as employment assistance and training free of charge. Incentives would also be given to assist the unemployed to start their own economic activities. If the laid-off formal employees became self-employed as a result, they would be allowed to use the unemployment benefits in advance in a lump sum. Enterprises which employed more than 30 laid-off formal employees would be eligible to apply for loans at a low interest rate from the unemployment insurance funds for a sum of 1,000 yuan per laid-off formal employee. Preferential taxation policies would also be introduced to promote the establishment of enterprises for the purpose of re-employing the laid-off formal employees.

To facilitate the re-employment of laid-off formal employees, adjustments were made in the local labour policy. Enterprises were allowed to 'borrow' surplus workers on a temporary basis, without taking up the responsibility of providing the benefits as embodied in the previous employment relationship. If the 'borrowed' worker received less than the average local wage from the new employer, the old enterprise would be obliged to pay the differences as a kind of living allowance for 3 to 6 months. Labour departments at different levels were required to set up data pools for surplus workers so as to facilitate labour force mobility throughout the city.

In 1996, the Guangzhou government issued 'Announcement for the Implementation of Re-employment Programmes'. Other than re-emphasizing previous policies, further measures were introduced to assist workers to seek employment on their own efforts and to provide them with the necessary social support. For example, it was a target that the re-employment rate should reach over 70 per cent, while the unemployment rate be contained within 3 per cent. It was also a core objective of the re-employment programmes to provide employment for laid-off or surplus employees, who showed a strong desire to find work, within a period of not over 6 months.

In specific terms, the 1996 regulations contained three measures to promote re-employment of laid-off formal employees.

First, enterprises, especially those in the tertiary sector, would be developed and expanded to absorb the unemployed and laid-off formal employees. Concerned departments were required to provide support for such enterprises, as well as the private business set up by the unemployed or the laid-off formal employees. Preferences in taxation, bank loans and administration fees were also applicable to enterprises with a certain percentage of their employees being laid-off formal employees or the unemployed.

Second, preferential policies were designed to support laid-off formal employees and the unemployed to establish economic units voluntarily. In addition to a lump-sum prepayment of unemployment benefits and medical fees, each unemployed worker would be given 300 yuan of 'start' fees for them to use as working capitals if they engaged in voluntarily organized economic activities. If an unemployed or laid-off formal employee had special difficulty in raising money for the purpose of starting their own economic activities, they would be eligible for a loan between 3,000 to 5,000 yuan and at low interest rates. For people who had been off work for over 12 months, and had the desire to work again, the Labour Department would issue an 'unemployment certificate with special difficulties' for them. With this certificate, the unemployed or laid-off formal employees would enjoy a variety of preferential treatments, such as immediate business registration, priority in the allocation of business stands, exemption or reduction in taxes and administration fees, reimbursement of 50 to 70 per cent of training fees to a maximum of 500 yuan, free employment information service, and free employment assistance on three occasions.

Third, various preferential policies were also developed to encourage enterprises to absorb and employ laid-off formal employees and the unemployed. If an enterprise employed an unemployed worker or a laid-off formal employee with an employment contract of more than two years, the Labour Department would appropriate to the enterprise concerned the remaining unemployment benefits entitled by the worker in a lump sum. The Labour Department would also allot to the enterprise 300 yuan of arrangement fees for each unemployed worker employed. But if the enterprise terminated the contract ahead of time, it must return the arrangement fees to the Labour Department. Similarly, if an enterprise had employed a laid-off formal employee from another enterprise with an employment contract of more than two years, the enterprise from where the laid-off formal employee came was required to provide arrangement fees for the employing enterprise, with the amount being settled between the two enterprises. Profit-making enterprises, which had merged, rented, or purchased enterprises that were either closed down or declared bankrupt were encouraged to continue to employ workers of the acquired enterprises. Arrangement fees for these workers could be deducted from the acquisition prices, again to be settled between the two enterprises.

Since 1998, the responsibility for helping the laid-off formal employees has increasingly been taken away from the enterprises. Strategies employed to deal with the laid-off formal employees have changed to emphasize the following.

First, laid-off formal employees would individually be encouraged to seek employment through either individual initiatives or the labour market. The Guangzhou government would promote the re-employment of laid-off formal employees through mobilizing the various government organs and mass organizations to provide help.

Second, the newly created Department of Industrial and Commercial Administration was required to design preferential policies for laid-off formal employees who started business on their own. The trade unions would be responsible for providing help and relief for laid-off formal employees who were in particularly poor economic conditions. Street offices and residents' committees would also be encouraged to provide help for laid-off formal employees in need of assistance, helping them to get re-employed, and developing various community-based services to support them. In addition, the Civil Affairs Department would be responsible for providing relief for the urban poor below the poverty line, and the Women's Federation would be required to provide help for female laid-off formal employees.

Third, to widen the support provided by the society, more liberal employment incentives would be developed to encourage both enterprises and individuals to help laid-off formal employees. Arrangement fees provided to enterprises providing employment for laid-off formal employees were adjusted to 600 yuan for a male laid-off formal employee aged 26 to 32 and a female aged 26 to 30, 800 yuan for a male aged 33 to 44 and a female aged 31 to 39, and 1,000 yuan for a male over 45 and a female over 40, provided that the number of the recruited laid-off formal employees was over 10 at one time. Employment assistance agencies or individuals that had helped the laid-off formal employees to get re-employed would receive 300 yuan for each successful case. An enterprise which had employed an laid-off formal employee for more than a year were also able to get financial reward at not more than 1,000 yuan for providing training for the re-employed worker.

One can thus conclude that the Guangzhou government has indeed worked hard to solve the problem of surplus labour. It shows particular concern about the unemployment rate as it knew the unemployment insurance fund, accumulated at 1 per cent of the wage bill, would simply be insufficient to support the surplus workers, estimated at about 30 per cent of the labour force, should they all become unemployed. In fact, the Guangzhou city was already fortunate in that its economy has so far not suffered any major set-back since economic reforms started and new jobs are generally available. Other cities with a higher unemployment rate and a less buoyant economy would have greater difficulties in preventing their unemployment insurance funds from going into the red.

Controlling the Influx of Non-local Workers

The phenomenon of migrant workers has for a long time caused grave concern for the Guangzhou government. Apart from the problem of public security, the Guangzhou government was also worried by the fact that the non-local workers often took away employment opportunities from local residents. As compared with local residents, migrant workers generally asked for lower wages, and employers were not required to provide them with medical and other social insurance benefits. For many years, the Guangzhou government has been making efforts to put the number of migrant workers under control. In the 1986 'Temporary Regulations on the Recruitment of Non-local Labourers in Guangzhou', enterprises or individual employers were required to register their non-local workers with the Labour Department. In 1990, the Guangzhou government issued 'Regulations on People Residing Temporarily in Guangzhou', according to which non-local workers were required to obtain employment license from the Labour Department.

The control of the non-local labourers became an urgent issue in the mid-1990s when the unemployed and laid-off formal employees were increasing in number and pressed the Guangzhou government to provide employment. The Labour Department was again put in charge of formulating policies for controlling and limiting the number of non-local workers. In Document 115 of 1996 issued by the Guangzhou government, labour departments at various levels were given the responsibility to control and limit the number of non-local workers. The result was that local laid-off formal employees and the unemployed would be given priority in employment opportunities before non-local workers; current non-local workers would cease to be employed at the end of the labour contract if their positions could be replaced by local workers. Enterprises could recruit a certain percentage of non-local workers after they had satisfied the needs of the locally unemployed for jobs. Enterprises that employed non-local workers were required to pay, according to local regulations, a certain amount of employment compensation fees or 'labour adjustment fees'.

At the end of 1997, the number of non-local workers in Guangzhou stood at over 700,000. The Labour Department has since then been issuing guidelines specifying the types of employment for which enterprises were not allowed to recruit non-local workers, or only allowed to recruit non-local workers at a certain percentage, or for which no restriction was imposed. In 1997, the Labour Department specified 23 types of employment for which enterprises were allowed to employ only 60 per cent of non-local workers, and also a number of employment types for which enterprises were not allowed to use non-local workers.

In 1998, the labour adjustment fees, paid by employers employing non-local workers, were adjusted to 11 yuan per non-local worker from outside the province and 7 yuan from within the province. In sectors and for types of employment for which employment of non-local workers was either forbidden or limited by the Labour Department, enterprises were to pay 2 per cent of the total wages of the non-local workers if they were employing non-local workers or if the number of non-local workers exceeded the limit.

In controlling the influx of non-local workers, the Guangzhou government has also been pressing enterprises to lay off current non-local workers, and refill the positions by local workers. In 'Suggestions on Enterprises Reducing Workers due to Economic Factors' issued by the Labour Department in May 1998, enterprises which had severe economic difficulties and met the conditions specified by the Labour Department were allowed to reduce the number of employees working for them. If they had employed non-local workers, they were required to first replace the non-local workers by local workers when they were cutting down the number of workers, and were not allowed to dismiss local workers who were willing to take up the positions of the non-local workers.

Re-employment Funds and Employment Service Centres

Other than controlling the influx of migrant workers, the Guangzhou government set up in 1996 're-employment funds' to further assist the surplus workers. The funding would come from the following six sources:

1. Earmarked appropriations for re-employment programmes by municipal and district governments at an annual basis.
2. The contribution for unemployment insurance will increase from 0.7 per cent of the wage bill to 1 per cent; the workers will pay the additional 0.3 per cent.
3. A sum of three times the wage bill in the previous year will be taken from the clearing accounts of enterprises that have either closed down or been declared bankrupt.
4. Enterprises contribute 0.3 per cent of the wage bill to set up training funds.
5. 40 per cent of the unemployment insurance funds available for municipal adjustment will be allocated to the re-employment funds.
6. Labour adjustment fees collected from enterprises using non-local workers for purposes controlled or limited by the Labour Department.

The re-employment funds thus set up were designed to support the unemployed and the laid-off formal employees to start economic activities and to attend training, as well as to provide financial support for enterprises which had recruited the unemployed and laid-off formal employees. At the end of 1997, more than 30 million yuan of re-employment funds had been accumulated.

In 1997, another effort was made to set up re-employment service centres to assist the surplus and laid-off formal employees, after a policy was passed by the central government to shift the relevant responsibility from individual enterprises to the society as a whole. According to the 'Announcement for the Establishment of Various Re-employment Service Centres' issued by the Guangzhou government in 1997, a three-level re-employment service programme was introduced at the municipal, industrial sector and enterprise levels. While one re-employment service centre would be established at the municipal level, industrial sectors and enterprises with surplus workers reaching over 5 per cent of the total labour force would be required to establish re-employment service centres and stations respectively.

The purpose of the re-employment centres or stations was to provide employment services for laid-off formal employees, while the labour relationship between the enterprises and the employees remained the same. Specifically, the re-employment service centres would be responsible for providing temporary 'trustee-administration' for the laid-off formal employees who had difficulties in getting re-employed due to disadvantages in ability or skills. It was further stated that the municipal re-employment service centre would be charged with the responsibility to help design measures governing the administration of surplus workers, collection and using of funds, and providing guidelines for centres established at the district, county and sector levels. Centres set up by industrial sectors would be responsible for designing and implementing re-employment programmes for surplus workers within individual sectors. The re-employment service stations at the enterprise level would be responsible for paying social insurance contributions on behalf of the employees, delivering living allowances and medical fees, and administering employment termination and retirement procedures for surplus workers under their trusteeship.

The maximum period for laid-off formal employees to receive assistance from the re-employment service stations under the trustee arrangement would be two years. During this period, the stations would help the laid-off formal employees go back to work as quickly as possible. Re-employed laid-off formal employees would then disassociate from the stations and terminate their status with the enterprises to which they originally belonged. If the laid-off formal employees refused to accept jobs introduced by the stations twice, the stations would either cease to deliver them living allowances or terminate the benefits they enjoyed with their enterprises. At the end of the two-year trustee period, laid-off formal employees who remained unemployed would terminate their status with their employing enterprises, and would be required to look for jobs in the open market.

Consolidating Protection for Surplus and Laid-off Formal Employees

It has been mentioned at the beginning of this book that in March 1998 Premier Zhu Rongji announced the decision of the central government to quicken the reform of the SOEs so that they could become profitable within 3 years. However, it would imply a greater number of workers would have to be laid off by the SOEs and that further support measures would be necessary. Responding to the announcement, the Guangzhou government refined its programmes for the surplus and laid-off formal employees. Before 1998, surplus workers who failed to find new employment were allowed to remain temporarily within their enterprises waiting for assignments. They would continue to receive wages at a reduced rate, with a minimum equal to the living allowances given to low-income workers. In 1998, the standard was revised to the lowest level of the unemployment benefits, around 35 per cent of the average local wage.

The second refinement was the dismissal of surplus workers. In Document 103 of 1994, the Guangzhou government laid down the regulation that surplus workers dismissed by their enterprises would receive various social insurance benefits, including unemployment benefits, workers' compensation, medical services, and retirement pensions. The 1994 Document also regulated the number of workers to be dismissed. If the number of surplus workers to be dismissed in one time amounted to over 20, enterprises were required to first explain the situation to all workers and the trade unions, and then report to the Labour department before enacting the decision. Enterprises were also obliged to give priority to the dismissed workers over others with compatible skills when they recruited workers within the next 6 months.

In 1998, this regulation was revised in that enterprises dismissing more than 20 workers in one time would have to consult the workers to be dismissed and the trade unions 30 days ahead of time. They would then have to submit detailed plans to the Labour Department, which possessed the final authority over the decision. If the Labour Department rejected the plan, enterprises would have to continue to employ the workers. There were also certain categories of workers, such as the disabled and pregnant, and those who would soon retire, whose employment would be protected. The purpose was to ensure that workers would be dismissed in an orderly manner and reduce the degree of instability.

A strategy based on the 'four lines of security-net' principle was also established to protect the surplus and laid-off formal employees. The first line of protection was the implementation of the minimum wage in enterprises, set at 380 yuan per month. The second line was the living allowances for laid-off employees, at a floor of 340 yuan per month. The third line was the unemployment insurance, ranging from 340 to 437 yuan per month. The last line was the relief for poor urban residents with per capita family income below 240 yuan.

In addition, 'employee poverty alleviation funds' were established at both the municipal and district levels to provide temporary financial help for workers who had difficulties in maintaining a basic living. Since 1998, laid-off formal employees would each be given a 'laid-off formal employees certificate', or a 'laid-off formal employees with special difficulties certificate', according to their individual situations. With these certificates, laid-off formal employees could receive various preferences such as reduced school fees for their children and housing rebates.

Lastly, the Guangzhou government refined its policy regarding the re-employment of surplus workers. Over the years, the goal adopted was to promote, as far as possible, the re-employment of laid-off employees by introducing various employment assistance programmes. However, with enterprises dismissing more and more employees to make themselves profitable, efforts to persuade enterprises to keep their surplus workers became rather futile. Accepting the fact that the chance for surplus and laid-off workers to get re-employed would decrease, the Guangzhou government has revised the preferential policies for their re-employment, such as reducing school fees for their children. In other words, more surplus and laid-off employees would become formally unemployed and greater use would be made of the unemployment insurance funds to assist them. The result was that contributions to unemployment insurance would have to be increased to keep the funds solvent.

There is still no conclusion as to the future development of unemployment insurance in Guangzhou. However, if the aim of the economic reform is to turn the SOEs into modern enterprises, preparation must then be made for a higher percentage of unemployment, as it is no longer possible for the SOEs to keep their surplus workers. The unemployment insurance system must also thoroughly be revised so that it can truly serve the unemployed.

Compensation for Work-related Injuries and Death

The compensation for disability and death of workers arising from industrial or work-related accidents is often the first insurance scheme established in other countries, but such provisions are not necessary in China as long as the enterprises are responsible for the welfare of their employees. Hence, only when SOEs are required to become modern enterprises, with the ability to make profits, that there is a need to take away the duty of compensation away from the enterprises. This explains why a municipal pool for disability and death of workers due to industrial or work-related accidents was not established in Guangzhou until 1993, one of the first cities in China to have such a scheme.

Contributions to the compensation pool for the participating enterprises ranged from 0.5 to 1.5 per cent of the wage bill. District social insurance companies were responsible for collecting the contributions, and the municipal social insurance company was in charge of unifying the management of the funds across the municipality. In 1997, several adjustments were made in benefit standards and the way enterprises made their contributions. As a result, compensations for industrial death and disability were divided into three main categories:

1. Benefits provided during the medical treatment period, which include medical expenses, nursing fees, meal subsidies, and living allowances.
2. Disability benefits, which include medical treatment, lump-sum disability compensation, disability pension, nursing fees, charge for supportive and rehabilitation apparatuses, and relocation subsidies.
3. Compensations for death and benefits for survivors, which include funeral expenses, lump-sum death compensation, and living allowances for dependents.

According to the 1993 regulations issued by the Labour Department (Labour Department of Guangzhou, 1993, pp. 290-306), medical fees for workers were to be shared between the enterprise and the social insurance company; with the enterprise providing 30 per cent and the pool supplying the rest 70 per cent of the costs. If there was no resulting disability, the enterprise alone would bear the medical costs. The enterprise was also required to provide an amount of living allowance for the worker, at least equal to the average wage of the worker in the last twelve months prior to the injury. If the worker was in need of nursing in at least two of the five daily activity items (eating, turning over the body, using the toilet, dressing, and moving about), he or she would receive from the enterprise an amount of nursing fee not less than the average local wage. Costs in purchasing supportive and rehabilitation apparatuses, such as artificial limbs, wheels or other necessary materials, were also to be shared between the enterprise and the municipal pool in the same arrangement as that for medical costs.

After medical treatment, workers who were judged as meeting disability standards would become eligible for a variety of disability or death compensations, including lump-sum disability compensation, disability pension, and disability nursing fees. These payments were all provided by social insurance companies according to the severity of disability, which was divided into ten grades in descending order. The amount of lump-sum disability compensation ranged from 15 months of the average local wage for workers with disability falling into Grade 1 to 6 months for those falling into Grade 10.

Disability pensions were provided on a monthly basis for local workers with disability falling into Grade 1 through Grade 4, which was respectively 85, 81, 78 and 75 per cent of the average monthly wage of the disabled worker in the previous year. If the average individual wage was lower than the average local wage, the local wage would be used as the base for calculating the pension payment. If the individual wage was higher than the local wage, the amount of the individual wage in excess of 150 per cent of the local wage would not be included into the base for calculating the benefit (*Labour Department of Guangzhou Annual Report 1993*, p. 295). Finally, disability pensions would be indexed to local wage increases, and adjustments would be made in June of each year (*Labour Department of Guangzhou Annual Report 1992*, pp. 458-70).

Disability nursing fees were provided on a monthly basis, with the amount being determined by the extent of care needed by the disabled workers. A worker in need of care in all of the five items of daily activities would receive 60 per cent of the average local wage, and a worker in need of care in four items would receive 50 per cent of the average local wage. In descending scale, the amount of nursing fees would decrease in the same proportion with each decrease in the number of items in which the worker needed nursing care.

Non-local workers with disability of Grades 1 through 7 were provided with lump-sum industrial injury compensations, the amount of which varied with the grades of disability. Those with disability falling into Grade 1 and Grade 2 would receive a lump-sum compensation equal to 13 years of the average local wage, and workers with disability of Grade 3 and Grade 4 would be given a lump-sum compensation equal to 12 years of the average local wage. Those with disability of Grades 5 through 7 were eligible for lump-sum compensations if enterprises were unable to arrange for them regular payments due to factors such as bankruptcy or closures. The amount of this compensation was set as 17, 16, and 15 years of 40 per cent of the average local wage respectively (*Labour Department of Guangzhou Annual Report 1993*, pp. 296-7).

When enterprises declared themselves bankrupt or were closed down, they were required to arrange for their workers with disability of Grades 5 through 7 by setting aside or providing a lump-sum equal to 15 years of 40 per cent of the average wage for each worker. For local workers, the money would be transferred to the social insurance company, which would be responsible to deliver the payment to the workers on a monthly basis until they reached retirement age, and then this compensation would be replaced by retirement pensions. Workers who resumed work before they reached the retirement age would cease to receive disability compensations.

Disabled workers with disability of Grades 8 through 10 would continue to be employed by their enterprises. However, if they were to be dismissed due to economic factors, they would receive lump-sum compensations from the enterprises according to the grades of their disability. The amount of the compensation was set at 8 months of the average individual wage in the previous year for workers with disability of Grade 8, 7 months of the wage for workers with disability of Grade 9, and 6 months for disabled workers of Grade 10.

Death and survivors' compensations included funeral expenses, lump-sum death compensations, and living allowances for survivors. The social insurance company provided these payments. The amount of funeral fees for workers who died as a result of industrial injury was equal to 4 months of the average local wage, and this sum would be delivered either to the working unit, which sponsored the funeral, or relatives of the deceased. The amount of lump-sum death compensation was equal to 20 months of the average local wage, which would be delivered to close relatives in order of inheritance sequence.

Living allowances for survivors were another major compensation for workers who died in relation to industrial injury, including workers who died due to diseases during retirement. This money was to be provided to the dependents of the deceased worker on a monthly basis, the amount of which varied with the number and types of dependents. For dependents that were urban residents, one dependent would receive 30 per cent of the average local wage, two dependents would get 50 per cent; and dependents that were single elders or orphans would get 60 per cent. Dependents who were rural residents would get a lower amount of compensation, which ranged between 21 and 42 per cent of the average local wage, taking into consideration also the need of single elders and orphans.

Amendments to Compensations in 1995

In 1995, several adjustments were made in the compensating system for workers injured in industrial accidents or work-related activities (*Labour Department of Guangzhou Annual Report 1995*, pp. 205-209). Disability benefits were generally raised in different degrees. Lump-sum disability compensations were increased from 15 to 24 months of the average local wage for workers with disability falling into Grade 1, from 14 to 22 months for those with disability falling into Grade 2, and from 13 to 20 months for workers with disability of Grade 3. In descending scale, each decrease in disability grades was accompanied by a decrease of two months' average wage. Lump-sum injury compensations were extended to cover contract and temporary workers with disability falling into Grades 8 through 10 upon the termination of the employment contract. The amount of the compensation would be equal to 10 months of the average local wage for workers with disability of Grade 8, 8 months of the average wage for workers with disability of Grade 9, and 6 months for workers with disability of Grade 10. This payment would be shared between the social insurance company and enterprises on a half-and-half basis.

Disability pensions and nursing fees were also increased. Disability pensions were increased from 85 per cent to 90 per cent of the average individual wage in the 12 months prior to the injury for workers with disability of Grade 1, from 81 to 85 per cent for workers with disability of Grade 2, and from 78 to 80 per cent for workers with disability of Grade 3. Workers with disability of Grade 4 continued to get 75 per cent. Individual wages in excess of 200 per cent of the average local wage would not be included into the base for calculating disability pensions. Nursing fees were increased from 60 to 70 per cent of the average local wage for workers in need of nursing care in all of the five items of daily activities, from 50 to 60 per cent for workers needing care in four items, from 40 to 50 per cent for workers needing nursing care in three items, and from 30 to 40 per cent for those needing care in two items.

Increases were also made in the death and survivors' compensations. The amount of lump-sum funeral fees was increased from 4 to 6 months of the average local wage. The lump-sum industrial death compensation was increased from 20 to 48 months of the average local wage. Beneficiaries included parents, spouse, children, and siblings in order of inheritance sequence. Living allowances for survivors were also adjusted according to types of dependents. A spouse would get 40 per cent of the average local wage on a monthly basis; other relatives would get 30 per cent; and single elders and orphans would receive 130 per cent. For dependents that were non-local urban residents, lump-sum payments would be provided out of the municipal pool.

In 1995, improvement was also made with regard to enterprise contributions. In particular, based on the ratio of the contributions and expenses for workers' compensation in individual enterprises, the contribution rates of enterprises would be floating around the ratio, and an awarding system was established. The contribution rates of enterprises would be reduced if the ratio was below 60 per cent, unchanged if between 61-70 per cent, and raised if above 71 per cent. The decreasing rates ranged from 30 to 5 per cent of the contributions of individual enterprises, and the increasing rates ranged from 35 to 3 per cent (Table 11.3). For instance, if an enterprise's original contribution rate was 1 per cent, and its expense/contribution ratio was 21 per cent, this enterprise would be given a 20 per cent decrease in its contribution. Decreasing rates were also accompanied by a monetary award system. The awarding rate was based on contributions, and the award would be directly allotted to enterprises, which could then use it to provide bonuses for staff or departments in charge of industrial security and sanitation.

Table 11.3: The floating rate and the awarding system for workers' compensation in Guangzhou

Ratio (%)	Floating rates (%)	Awarding rate (%)
10 and below	-30	10
11-20	-25	9
21-30	-20	8
31-40	-15	7
41-50	-10	6
51-60	-5	5
61-70	No change	
71-75	+3	
76-85	+5	
86-90	+8	
91-100	+10	
101-120	+15	
121-130	+20	
131-140	+25	
141-150	+30	
150 and above	+35	

Source: 'Department of Labour of Guangzhou, 1995', p. 209.

At the end of 1995, the compensation pool covered 950,400 workers, about 40 per cent of the active urban labour force in Guangzhou.

Maternity Insurance

The latest employment insurance established in Guangzhou was the new maternity insurance scheme set up in 1995 in response to 'Ministry of Labour Trial Regulations on Maternity Insurance for Employees in Enterprises of 1994' (Document 504), which is the most important document governing this programme. Like most of the regulations issued by the central government during the reform period, Document 504 set forth only some broad principles requiring local governments to establish maternity insurance pooling for employees in urban enterprises. One of the objectives of this programme was to redistribute the financial burdens of enterprises over providing maternity benefits for employees. Under the old labour insurance regulations, maternity benefits were provided solely by individual enterprises. Enterprises with different numbers and proportions of female employees would thus differ widely in the amount of expenses for this welfare benefit. To balance the burdens across enterprises, the programme was designed to be funded solely by enterprise contributions based on the total wages, and a ceiling of 1 per cent of the wage bill was set for the contribution rate. Local governments were given authority to design specific policies regarding the exact contribution rate, and the levels of benefits based on individual local conditions.

Based on the general principles contained in Document 504 of 1994, the Labour Department of Guangzhou designed specific methods to implement the regulations issued in 1995 (*Labour Department of Guangzhou Annual Report 1995*, p. 211). The pool was designed to cover all types of enterprises and employees in Guangzhou except for permanent employees in government organs and public institutions. Contribution rates were set at 0.7 per cent of the total wages of each participating enterprise in the previous year. Benefits would include subsidies during maternity leave, medical subsidies, lump-sum nutrition subsidies, and wage leave for spouse. Maternity leave subsidies were provided according to the number of leave days, which were the average monthly wage of employees in individual enterprises in the previous year divided by 30 for each leave day. Medical subsidies, which covered expenses for medical examination, child delivering, hospitalization, medicine, and medical treatment during maternity leave, were 1,600 yuan for normal birth-giving, 2,400 yuan for difficult and multiple birth, and 300-1,600 yuan for abortion according to the months of pregnancy. The amount of lump-sum nutrition subsidy was 25 per cent of the average monthly wage for normal birth-giving, and 50 per cent for difficult and multiple birth. Finally, a 10 to 15 day wage leave was available for spouses. The social insurance company through enterprises provided all these benefits to the workers.

PART FOUR

A LONG AND WINDING ROAD OF SOCIAL SECURITY REFORM

12 Has China Established a Socialist Social Security System with Chinese Characteristics?

Pay-as-you-go to Funded Social Security

The positive results of the reforms that China has been carrying out in its social security system since the mid-1980s have widely been acknowledged. The reforms have resolved, to a large extent, the problem of enterprise-insurance that has characterized the system before the reform period. Workers are now, at least, ensured of some form of payments when they retire, become unemployed or injured, and what is important is that these payments are no longer related, as in the past, to the financial vicissitudes of their employing enterprises.

So far as reforms in old-age pensions are concerned, a new system consisting of social pooling and individual accounts is now in existence as a valid alternative to meeting the income security needs of the urban retirees. However, problems still remain for workers who have already retired or are approaching retirement age, as they simply would not have enough to support themselves in old age. The financing of pensions for this transitional cohort failing to build up their own individual accounts is thus the major social security problem that China has to resolve in future.

Policy-makers in China have generally viewed the financing of pension obligations for the transitional workers as a technical problem, and have left it to the actions of local governments. It is, however, obvious that the existing pension funds have already incurred considerable liabilities to both old and new workers and there is little likelihood that they can ever fulfill their promises to the full. The situation is further complicated by the fact that savings in individual accounts of the new workers in most localities are only notional, as fully funded individual accounts are often regarded as unnecessary.

As the case in Guangzhou shows, local governments have often used the savings in the individual accounts to offer generous pension payments, hoping that more workers in the non-public sector would join. It is assumed that with the extension of the coverage, increased contributions will then be sufficient to cover the deficits. But this practice has no doubt made the individual accounts unreal and there is also no guarantee that the workers would have their savings back when they retire. In other words, although pension reforms in China have been emphasizing individual savings for their own old age, the new pension system remains to be pay-as-you-go.

The transition from a pay-as-you-go system to a fully or partially funded system is a challenge for all nations undertaking such a transition as substantial increases in the payroll tax are required from the present generation of the working population. The challenge is even greater for China, as the government there it has not only reformed its social security system, but has also been turning, at the same time, its economy from the former planned system to a market-oriented one. Hence, other than supporting a rapidly increasing number of retirees, the new social security system has also to provide for the surplus and laid-off employees, who accounted for about one-third of the urban labour force. These two burdens added together have thus made reforms of the social security system in China extremely difficult, if not impossible.

The prolonged decline in the economic performance of the SOEs in the later part of the 1990s, which is the result of a shift of economic vigor from the public to the non-public sector, has made the situation worse. A consequence of which is that the Chinese government has been forced to place more emphasis on the political effects of the reforms rather than the income protection functions of the social security system itself. Short-term stability and continuity became thus the goals of recent social security reforms, while long-term viability and feasibility were often temporarily put aside or simply neglected.

It is thus difficult to say whether or not China has succeeded in constructing a socialist social security system with Chinese characteristics. As mentioned in the beginning of this book, the Chinese leaders have never bothered to give an explanation to the meaning of 'a socialist social security system with Chinese characteristics'. What one can say for most is that China has learnt the hard lesson that the labour insurance system, borrowed from the Soviet Union and enacted in 1951, was totally unsuitable for China, given particularly the level of economic development that the country had experienced. What China has achieved in bringing in the reforms is to construct a system that is at least compatible with the form of economy that the country has been establishing.

Whither Social Security in China Might Go?

At a time when China is still on its way to refining its economic and legal structure, the dismantling of the planned economy has not only created a mounting need for income protection, but has also weakened the apparatus and mechanism of the government for meeting these needs. Specifically, it means that the public ownership sector, which has all along been playing a dominant role in the urban economy, is no longer able to meet the social security needs of its employees. The only way to rescue the newly established social insurance funds, largely made up of contributions from SOEs from going into deficit, is to spread the burden to a wider spectrum of economic units, particularly the private enterprises. However, notwithstanding the fact that China is a socialist country, it is no longer possible for the government to dictate what enterprises in the non-public sector have to do, unless China is prepared to give up its decision to go for a market economy.

Shrinkage in the scope of coverage, side by side with high economic growth, forms therefore the most urgent social security problem that China has to tackle. As the situation in Guangzhou shows, the decline in the number of covered employees, from 1 million in 1996 to 0.6 million in 1998, was attributed to the diminishing role of the SOEs and the corresponding growth of the private sector. Hence, unless drastic measures are made in the near future to extend the social security coverage to include employees in the private sector, the social security system in China will soon come to a dead end.

However, an expansion of social security coverage to the private sector is easier said than done as it involves a significant redistribution of resources. The aim of the economic reforms, as discussed in this book, is an effort of the government to turn the SOEs into independent economic entities. In other words, SOEs must separate themselves from the government and raise their productivity. But as long as the SOEs are still carrying their social obligations inherited from the planned economy era, there is little chance for them to survive in the open market. The only way to make the SOEs competitive is to have their welfare burdens shared by the entire society. But for a country that has for a long time perceived the provision of social security as a symbol of socialist superiority, and has taken it as a government responsibility, it is certainly not easy now to persuade the people that it is a burden that should be shared by all.

Appendix

A Chronological Account of the Development of Social Security in China

1922 August

The Secretariat of the Chinese Labour Association issued the "Labour Insurance Outline." Article 11 stated that female manual workers should be entitled to 8 weeks maternity leave and other female workers to 6 weeks. Female workers on maternity leave should be paid their normal wages.

1925 May

The All-China Federation of Labour at its second meeting passed a resolution to call for the formulation of labour laws, including the provisions for social insurance (item no. 5).

1927 June

The All-China Federation of Labour at its fourth meeting passed a "resolution on economic struggle" which demanded the provisions for free medical care, paid sickness leave for up to 3 months, benefits for injured workers and the retired, assistance for their dependants, and payments for workers leaving their jobs.

1928

The Kuomintang government pronounced an intention to formulate a labour insurance law.

1930 June

The General Assembly of representatives of the Republic of Chinese Soviets passed the "Labour Protection Law" which included social insurance regulations.

1931 December

The Central Executive Committee of the Republic of Chinese Soviets promulgated the "Labour Law of the Republic of Chinese Soviets," which included social insurance.

1934

The Department of Industry of the Kuomintang government produced a draft labour insurance law, which the government adopted in 1937 as one of its tasks for implementation.

1948 July

The All-China Federation of Labour at its sixth meeting passed "A Resolution on the Immediate Tasks of the Labour Movement in China," which included suggestions to introduce labour insurance to cover sickness, confinement, disablement, old age and death. The Resolution stated that the cost of providing the benefits would be borne by the factories, but their administration would be the joint responsibility of the factories and the trade unions.

1948 December

The North-East Executive Commission of the CCP promulgated the "Provisional War-Time Labour Insurance Regulations for State-Owned Enterprises in the North-East," which provided benefits relating to work accidents, sickness, retirement, confinement and death.

1950

The Chinese Political Consultative Assembly passed the "Common Guidelines." Article 32 stated that "... People's Government should fix minimum wages in different places according to situations of different trades, and should gradually introduce a labour insurance system."

1950 May

The Administration Council announced the "Directives Regarding Unemployed Workers." The Department of Labour promulgated the "Temporary Measures Regarding Unemployed Workers."

1951 February

The Administration Council of the People's Republic of China (PRC) promulgated the "Labour Insurance Regulations," which came into effect on March 1, 1951. It was applied to workers and staff employed in state-owned, joint state-privately operated, privately operated, or cooperative factories and mines, including their respective administrative organs and subordinate units, and in enterprises and their subordinate units involved in railways, navigation operations, and postal and telecommunications organizations that employed more than 100 workers and staff.

1952

The Administration Council of the PRC issued directives regarding health care for government workers at different levels of the People's Government, parties, organizations, and their subordinate units.

1953 January

The Administration Council of the PRC promulgated a revised version of the "Labour Insurance Regulations," extending the coverage to workers and staff employed in capital construction units of factories, mines and transport services, and state-owned construction enterprises.

1954 September

The right of the workers to welfare benefits was formally recognized in Articles 91 and 93 of the Constitution of the PRC adopted in September 1954.

1955 April and December

The State Council issued further regulations regarding the retirement, death, sickness, injury and confinement benefits for government workers.

1956

The coverage of the "Labour Insurance Regulations" was extended to those working in trade, commerce, the food industry, finance and civil aviation.

1958 March

The State Council promulgated "Provisional Regulations (Draft) Regarding the Retirement of Workers," giving retirement entitlement to workers and staff of state-owned and joint state-private enterprises and undertakings, government institutions and people's organizations.

1965

A social insurance plan was introduced for workers employed in urban industrial collectives.

1978 May

The State Council issued "Provisional Measures for the Protection of Aged, Infirm and Invalid Cadres" and "Provisional Measures for Workers upon Retirement and Leaving their Jobs." These two measures provided generous benefits for cadres and workers who had retired or left their jobs but were not qualified for retirement pensions.

1979 July

The Central Bureau of Labour sent out directives regarding the provision of pensions to workers who have retired or left their jobs.

1980 March

The Central Bureau of Labour and the All-China Federation of Trade Unions issued directives regarding the administration and financing of labour insurance and stipulated that the work could either be taken up by the enterprises concerned or the trade unions, or shared between the two.

1981 April

The State Council issued regulations regarding sickness leave of workers in government institutions.

1985 September

A draft proposal of the Central Committee of the CCP on the 7th Five - Year Plan with a chapter on social security was endorsed.

1985 October

It was announced that the government was in the process of drafting social insurance regulations for workers working on contract terms in special economic zones and in individual enterprises.

1986 April

The 7th Five - Year Plan for National Economic and Social Development with a chapter on social security was adopted at the 4th Meeting of the 6th National People's Congress.

1986 September

The State Council promulgated directives for the employment of new workers at state-owned enterprises on contract terms and for the setting up of unemployment insurance for workers dismissed or laid off by bankrupt enterprises.

1987 March

The State Council approved a proposal of the Ministry of Civil Affairs to introduce social security schemes in the villages.

1988 July

The Ministry of Labour sent out a "Circular on the Name and the Functions of Social Insurance Agencies," pointing out that social insurance agencies under the Ministry of Labour should uniformly be named as "Social Insurance Enterprise Management Bureau." Its responsibilities include the collection, management and payment of the enterprise workers' social insurance funds, as well as the maintenance of the relevant files.

1989 August

The Ministry of Health and the Ministry of Finance jointly announced a set of directives regarding the administration of medical reimbursement schemes for enterprise workers. The principles, the scope of coverage, the types of payments and the management of the schemes were spelt out in detail.

1989 September

The Ministry of Labour issued a "Temporary Decree on Labour Management in Individual Enterprises," specifying in Chapter 4 that individual enterprises should set up old age insurance funds for their workers. The contribution of the enterprises should be around 15% of the wage bill, while the contribution of workers should not exceed 3% of their own wages. Enterprises should also comply with the decrees and regulations regarding unemployment insurance, occupational insurance, medical care and other welfare benefits for the workers.

1991 June

The State Council issued a "Decision on the Reform of the Old Age Insurance System of Enterprise Workers." The three-tier old age insurance system for enterprise workers was formally adopted and implemented.

1992 January

The Ministry of Civil Affairs sent out a "Basic Proposal (Trial) on Old Age Insurance in the Villages at the County Level." The Proposal sets out the details of the old age insurance funds to be introduced in the villages.

1992 February

The Ministry of Agriculture announced a "Decree on Labour Management in Township Enterprises." Chapters 4 and 5 of the Decree specified that township enterprise workers should enjoy protection in old age, occupational insurance and medical care and other kinds of social insurance in accordance with government regulations.

1993 February

The Ministry of Labour expounded its ideas on the "Regulations Regarding the Change in the Operating Mechanism of State-Owned Enterprises," spelling out the procedures in establishing and perfecting the social insurance system.

1993 July

The Ministry of Labour issued a "Decree on the Management of Old Age Insurance Funds for Enterprise Workers."

1994 January

The State Council issued "Regulations on the Support Work of the Five Guarantees in the Villages." The Regulations recognized the support offered under the Five Guarantees as an important part of the social security system in the villages. They further specified the objectives, the target population, the content and the modes of operation of the Five Guarantees.

1994 April

The State Commission on Systems Reconstruction, the Ministry of Finance, Ministry of Labour and Ministry of Health jointly issued a circular on "Opinions on an Experiment to Reform the Enterprise Workers' Medical Care System." It was proposed that individual and risk-pooling accounts should be set up to form a medical insurance fund to meet the costs of health care.

1994 July

Labour Law of the PRC was adopted by the 8th Meeting of the 8th NPC Standing Committee, to be implemented as from January 1, 1995. The Law stipulated that the state has the responsibility to set up social insurance funds so that workers can have access to assistance and compensation in old age, illness, occupational injury, unemployment and maternity.

1994

The State Council announced a plan to tackle poverty up to the year 2000. The target was to provide the 80 million poor people in China with the means of a basic living by the end of the century.

1994 August

The Department of Foreign Trade and Economic Cooperation of the Ministry of Labour issued a set of regulations concerning labour management in foreign investment enterprises. Regulation no. 17 stated that foreign investment enterprises must comply with state decrees and join in social insurance funds on old age, unemployment, medical care, occupational injury and maternity.

1994 December

A demonstration health insurance project sponsored by the State Council began in Jiujiang and Zhenjiang, two medium-size cities on the Yangzi River in Jiangxi and Jiangsu Provinces.

1995 March

The State Council issued a "Circular on Deepening the Reform of the Old Age Insurance System for Enterprise Workers." The Circular laid down a separation of the administration of the old age insurance schemes from the management of the funds themselves, the setting up of supervisory committees, and the choice between two options in operating the individual and the risk-pooling accounts.

1996 March

The Fourth Session of the 8th NPC approved "The Nineth Five – Year Plan for National Economic and Social Development, 1996 – 2000" and adopted the proposal to speed up the reform of the old-age, unemployment and medical insurance systems and to establish a social security system that includes social insurance, social relief, social welfare, assistance to ex-servicemen, mutual help, and personal savings.

1996 August

The Ministry of Labour issues a circular regarding "Temporary Measures to Implement Work-Related Insurance for Enterprise Workers."

The 21st Meeting of the Standing Committee of the 8th NPC approved the "Law to Protect the Rights of the Elderly of the PRC."

1996 December

The State Council and the Central Committee of the CCP held a national health conference to discuss and examine major policy issues in health and later issued the "Decisions on the Health Reform and Development," endorsing the results of the experiment conducted in Jiujiang and Zhenjiang.

1997

The State Council issued "A Decision on Establishing a Unified Basic Old-Age Insurance System for Enterprise Workers," endorsing the idea of a three-tier income security system to protect old age.

1997 September

Party secretary-general Jiang Zemin announced at the First Session of the 15th Congress of the CCP the decision to reform the state-owned enterprises.

1998 March

The First Session of the 9th NPC approved the proposal to reform the state-owned enterprises and endorsed the necessity to perfect the social security system.

The Chinese Premier, Zhu Rongji, announced the formation of the Ministry of Labour and Social Security, putting under its administration all the social insurance programmes that were previously run by different ministries, including the old age insurance run by the Ministry of Civil Affairs among the peasants, medical insurance by the Department of Health and social insurance for workers in government institutions.

1998 August

The State Council issued "An Announcement to Establish a Unified Pension Plan at the Provincial Level," transferring sector-based pools to the responsibility of local administrations.

1999 January

The State Council issued "Temporary Regulations on Collecting Social Insurance Contributions," unifying the procedures for collecting contributions.

The State Council issued "Regulations on Unemployment Insurance," fixing an acceptable living standard for the unemployed and introduced measures to promote their re-employment opportunities.

1999 March

The newly created Ministry of Labour and Social Security announced three regulations to increase the administrative efficiency of social insurance. These three regulations are: "Temporary Measure to Regulate the Registration of Social Insurance" "Temporary Measure to Regulate the Declared Contribution of Social Insurance Fees" and "Measure to Supervise and Inspect the Contribution of Social Insurance Fees".

Bibliography

Cao, S. (1999), 'A Mistaken Prescription for Enterprises Declaring Bankruptcy', in *Hot Topics in China*, China Statistical Publishing House, Beijing, pp.160-1.

Chen, L. (1990), *Lessons on Social Security*, Beijing Knowledge Press, Beijing. (in Chinese)

China Civil Affairs Statistical Yearbook Editorial Committee, various years, *China Civil Affairs Statistical Yearbook*, China Statistical Press, Beijing. (in Chinese)

China Labour and Social Security Ministry (1999a), *Lectures on Social Security Administration*, The China Labour and Social Security Ministry Press, Beijing. (in Chinese)

China Labour and Social Security Ministry (1999b), *Issues of Top Priority: Instructions for Providing Basic Security and Re-employment Programme for the Laid-off Formal Employees in SOEs*, The Economic Science Press, Beijing. (in Chinese)

China Labour Statistical Yearbook Editorial Committee, various years, *China Labour Statistical Yearbook*, China Statistical Press, Beijing. (in Chinese)

China Statistical Yearbook Editorial Committee, various years, *China Statistical Yearbook*, China Statistical Press, Beijing. (in Chinese)

Chow, N. (1987), *The Administration and Financing of Social Security in China*, The Centre of Asian Studies, The University of Hong Kong, Hong Kong.

Chow, N. (2000), *Socialist Welfare with Chinese Characteristics*, The Centre of Asian Studies, The University of Hong Kong, Hong Kong.

Cui, N. (1988), 'Reflections on a Social Security System with Chinese Characteristics', *International Social Security Review*, vol.41, no.2, pp.170-5.

Davis, D. and Harrell, S. (eds.) (1993), *Chinese Families in the Post-Mao Era*, University of California Press, London.

Fu, H. and Li, F. (1994), *A Glossary of Social Insurance*, Henan People's Press, Henan. (in Chinese)

Guangdong Labour Bureau, Insurance and Welfare Office, various years, *Selected Documents on Labour Insurance*, Guangdong Labour Bureau, Guangzhou. (in Chinese)

Guangzhou Labour Department, various years, *Guangzhou Labour Department Annual Report*, Guangzhou Labour Department, Guangzhou. (in Chinese)

Guangzhou Statistical Yearbook Editorial Committee, various years, *Guangzhou Statistical Yearbook*, China Statistical Press, Beijing. (in Chinese)

Guo, J. (ed.) (1995), *An Overall Review of the Chinese Social Security System*, China Democracy and Legal System Press, Hebei. (in Chinese)

He, X. (1999), '1998-1999: Analysis and Prospects of Economic Reforms in China', in *The Social Blue Book: Analysis and Forecast of the Social Situation of China in 1999*, Social Sciences Literature Press, Beijing, pp.337-52. (in Chinese)

Ho, P. (1997), *Social Insurance in the Reform of State-owned Enterprises*, Economic Science Press. (in Chinese)

Hu, X. (1998), *China Social Insurance Towards the 21st Century*, The China Labour Press, Beijing. (in Chinese)

Kreieg, J. and Schadler, M. (eds.) (1994), *Social Security in the People's Republic of China*, Institut fur Asienkunde, Hamburg.

Leung, J. (1998), 'Social Security Reforms: A long and Winding Road', in J. Cheng (ed.), *China Review 1998*, The Chinese University Press, Hong Kong, pp.479-99.

Leung, J. and Nann, R. (1995), *Authority and Benevolence: Social Welfare in China*, The Chinese University Press, Hong Kong.

Lin, D., Shi, Z. and Zeng, F. (1996), *An Exploration of Old-age Insurance Models in Guangzhou*, Unpublished mimeograph.

Lo, T. and Cheng, J. (eds.) (1996), *Social Welfare Development in China: Constraints and Challenges*, Imprint Publications, Chicago.

Qiao, J. (1999), '1998-1999: The Situation of Employees in China', in *The Social Blue Book: Analysis and Forecast of the Social Situation of China in 1999*, Social Sciences Literature Press, Beijing, pp.427-50. (in Chinese)

Tang, J. (1995), *Market Economy and Social Security*, Heilongjiang People's Press, Harbin. (in Chinese)

Wang, D. (1999), *China Faces Unemployment*, The Economic Daily Press, Beijing. (in Chinese)

Wang, S. (1999), 'China Lacks Motivating Forces to Deepen SOEs Reforms', in *Hot Topics in China*, China Statistical Publishing House, Beijing, pp.145-9. (in Chinese)

White, G. (1998), 'Social Security Reforms in China: Towards an East Asian Model?', in G. White and H. Kwon (eds.), *The East Asian Welfare Mod*el, Routledge, London and New York, pp.175-98.

Wong, L. (1998), *Marginalization and Social Welfare in China*, Routledge, London and New York.

World Bank (1994), *Averting the Old Age Crisis: Politics to Protect the Old and Promote Growth*, World Bank Policy Research Series, Oxford University Press, New York.

World Bank (1997), *China 2020: Old Age Security*, World Bank, Washington, D.C.

Wu, L. (1996), *General Discussions on Social Security*, China Finance and Economics Press, Beijing. (in Chinese)

Zhang, H. (1998), '1997-8: The Situation of the Private Sector in China', in *The Social Blue Book: Analysis and Forecast of the Social Situation of China in 1998*, Social Sciences Literature Press, Beijing, pp.355-67. (in Chinese)

Zhang, H. (1999), '1998-9: The Situation of the Private Sector in China', in *The Social Blue Book: Analysis and Forecast of the Social Situation of China in 1999*, Social Sciences Literature Press, Beijing, pp.482-91. (in Chinese)

Zhang, M. and Zhou T. (1998), 'Reforms of Large and Medium-sized SOEs: Progress, Problems and Strategies of SOEs Reforms in 1997', in *Report of National Condition of China*, pp.154-161, Beijing: China Statistical Publishing House, Beijing, pp.154-61. (in Chinese)

Zhou, S. (1998), 'A Review of SOEs Reforms in China in the Past Two Decades and their Prospects', *China Social Sciences*, vol.6, pp.44-58. (in Chinese)

Zhu, Y. (1995), 'Major Changes Underway in China's Industrial Relations', *International Labour Review*, vol.134, no.2, pp.37-49.

Zhu, Y. (1999), '1998-9: The Situation and Prospects of SOEs Reforms in China', in *The Social Blue Book: Analysis and Forecast of the Social Situation of China in 1999*, Social Sciences Literature Press, Beijing, pp.123-46. (in Chinese)

Index